I0428574

How To Retire Happy & Secure

Everything you need to do to assure your happiness

David Rye

WESTERN PUBLICATIONS
10271 South 175th Avenue
Goodyear, AZ 85358-5502

1

CONTENTS

Introduction

If it is handled right, retirement can be one of the most exciting chapters in your life. However, if your retirement is not planned correctly, it can unravel and you could suddenly discover that you don't have enough money to continue living the lifestyle you've grown accustomed to. Sudden unexpected medical expenses, for example, can devastate your retirement savings.

How To Retire Happy & Secure is all you need to make sure you plan correctly and enjoy retirement. It's tailor-made for individuals who have a common goal: to retire in $tyle. It tells how to master the latest retirement fundamentals and techniques quickly, without wasting time chasing theoretical concepts. It's full of real-world examples and advice, supplemented with a rich menu of easy-to-use Web sites that offer a wealth of additional information. Filled with specific tips and abundant resources, this book is the quick-and-easy answers to your retirement concerns, including:

- How much money do you really need to retire?

- Is it better to sell your existing home and buy a cheaper one when retiring?

- What are your best investment options when you retire?

- How can you keep taxes from devouring your estate?

Chapter 1

Getting Started

You're on track to retire when you know where you're going and how you'll get there!

What do people who successfully retire have in common? They become financially independent before they retire and they are in the minority. According to the Social Security Administration, most Americans retire on less than $20,000 a year from their retirement savings accounts. These are people just like you, who worked hard all of their lives. The facts are that most people either lack the discipline or don't know how to save and invest their money. We'll help you get started in this chapter.

Achieving Financial Independence

Being financially independent means having the wherewithal to do whatever you want to do, regardless of the cost. Some would argue that only a few people in the world ever achieve the enviable position of truly being financially independent. Perhaps Bill Gates is one of them. We would argue that being financially independent is more dependent upon one's state of mind than it is on some arbitrary dollar figure. For example, you may have concluded that you would be happy and satisfied with a well-thought-out retirement plan that costs you X dollars to maintain and allows you the added luxuries you desire. Once you have accumulated the necessary dollars to maintain that plan, then you have achieved financial independence.

Achieving financial independence when you're up to your neck in debt may make the goal seem impossible to reach. Vow to become debt-free in a year and list the steps you'll take to make that happen. To learn more about becoming debt-free, pick up a copy of *Life Without Debt* by Bob Hammond. Some excellent resources are offered at a minimal cost or free to anyone who is interested in

11

becoming financially independent. A great website that offers a variety of articles pertaining to financial freedom is *www.money com*. Also consider a subscription to a monthly magazine such as *Fortune* or *Smart Money*. A couple of suggested books are *The* 9 *Steps to Financial Freedom* by Suze Orman or *The Six-Day Financial Makeover* by Robert Pagliarini.

To become financially independent, you must consistently save and invest your money. You need a savings plan that's flexible and most important, something you can stick to. Your first challenge will be to get control over your spending habits and establish a monthly budget for everything you buy. If you can start saving on even the little things, it will add up to big dollars over a relatively short period of time.

Make up a savings bill to yourself. When it comes time to pay the bills, make sure it's the first bill that gets paid, in the form of a deposit to your savings account. That way, adding money to your savings becomes a top priority. After you payoff all your bills and discover that you have some money left over, make another deposit to your savings account. Find out if your employer's payroll system allows you to make direct deposits into a savings account. If it does, sign up for the program today; in a short period of time, you won't even miss the money that's deducted from your paycheck. When you get unexpected money (e.g., a gift, a bonus, tax refunds), deposit it into your savings account so you won't use it to buy something you don't need.

Payoff your home mortgage faster by sending your payment coupons in early along with an extra payment. This is a wise financial move because you will be charged less interest due to the shortening of your overall home loan. Don't rush out to trade your car in just because the loan is paid off. There is nothing better than a car that's paid for. If "old faithful" is still running, keep it and save the money.

How Much Will You Need?

If for example, you decide you need $5,000 a month to cover your retirement expenses and the standard of living that you've grown accustomed to, how much will you need in your savings account? To determine how much you will need in your savings and investment accounts to provide you with an income of $5,000 a month, go to *Money* magazine's website at *www.money.cnn.com/retirement/index.html* and use the formula on the right-hand side of the Retirement home page. This will help you determine the amount you'll need to save each month in order to reach your goal.

You can't withdraw funds from a retirement account before your are 59 and a half without incurring a tax penalty? Even though the money is yours, if you withdraw any from your account prior to turning 59, the money will be subject to income taxes based on your current salary bracket and tax rate. There is also a mandatory 20 percent tax withholding deposit that is applied up front to the money being withdrawn. Not only will you face tax penalties, but you will also experience an early-withdrawal penalty, which is around 10 percent. Certain hardship exceptions are available for individuals in need, so if you get in a serious bind, consider looking into this in greater detail.

Most plans allow you to borrow up to 50 percent of what you have in your plan. If you need to borrow money, use this option only as a last resort. If you borrow from your plan and, for whatever reason, you can't pay it back, the money will come out of your plan to pay the loan. You'll be required to pay income tax on the withdrawal and the IRS will charge you a 10 percent early-withdrawal penalty.

Your Current Financial Status

To find out where you are financially, go through your checkbook and write down what you spent your money on over the past three months (e.g., food, entertainment, credit card interest, etc.). Some credit card companies categorize your purchases for you so that you can see your spending patterns. How much money did you make, and did you have enough to cover all of your expenses? Did you spend more than you made? Where did the money go? If you spent less than you made, what did you do with the extra money? Consider these steps to improve your current financial status:

Set financial goals. To be meaningful, a goal must be very specific, with a designated completion date assigned to it. For example, what are your spending and savings goals next month?

Cut back on expenses. If you are living above your means, figure out a way to live below your means. You must figure out how to live on what you make or you will never gain control of your finances.

Create a contingency fund. Your contingency fund should sufficiently cover three to six months of your expenses in case you become unemployed, your car breaks down, or something unexpected comes up.

A Budget is Essential

Everyone should have a budget, even millionaires. It is critical to understand where your money is coming from and where is it going after you retire. By monitoring your spending habits, you will begin to identify areas where cost savings can occur. Ultimately you will then be able to create a budget that is conducive to your retirement. It will become a tool that you can reference to keep your spending on track that contains your buying, spending, and saving habits. Find a good resource or tool that is available for you to implement right away. For example, if you go to Simple Planning has an excellent budget planning program that is downloadable at *www.simpfepfanning.net*. If you have Microsoft Office, then consider using the financial templates that are included in the program. Any financial planning tool will help organize your spending and make the process less demanding on your personal time.

After you complete your budget, you will start to see some money-saving areas within your personal realm that you can tackle right away. Identify what are necessary expenses and what are luxury expenses. For example, does each family member really need a cell phone? Do you truly need the glorified cable television package? Closely review your miscellaneous spending. Is there anything that you can do away with? Do you see any patterns in your spending behavior that you can begin to address? Prioritize your budget. Consider categorizing the most important to least important expenditures you have. Then begin assessing what you can do away with or cut back on. Be very realistic as to what your retirement expenses are expected to be.

What to Watch Out For

If you're spending every dime you make, what can I do to get my expenses under control before you retire? This is where your budget will really come in handy. Understanding your expenses and where they are coming from will be your first step in getting them under control. The budget will help you to outline your expenses and identify any areas that can be eliminated. For example, do you really need to have that Starbucks coffee every day? At $3 a day, that's $1,095 a year! Your budget will flag expenses that you can begin to think about reducing or eliminating.

You need to know what your expenses are today so that you can project what they will be when you retire. It will help with comparing what your expenses are today versus what they are projected to be in retirement. For example, one expense you have today might be your high gasoline bill that is necessary for commuting to your current job. However, after retirement, you won't be commuting so your gas cost should drop substantially. The same goes for things such as multiple phone lines and cell phones required for your current job. You may not need all of these services when you retire. Identifying these items now will help you forecast for your actual retirement expenditures.

Stop buying stuff you really don't need. There is always a "latest and greatest" for any product, and if this is your thing, then you'll pay for it. Let's look at televisions. In less than two years, plasma television prices have been cut in half. Another good example is the latest, hottest, fastest computer technology, which costs plenty at first but then plummets in price in a matter of months. What's key to avoiding debt is to hold off on any frivolous spending. Apply any extra money you may have toward paying off your debt before you decide to accumulate more debt. According to *Money* magazine's October 2005 issue, the average credit card debt per American household was $9,312. Avoid this trap by simply adhering to your budget.

Avoid credit and loan traps that can stifle your retirement. Inappropriate use of loans can become one of your biggest financial downfalls. When your wallet is nearly empty and your checkbook balance is low, you know you're nearing your spending limit. But if you can easily turn to credit, you are more likely to overspend without realizing it-until the bills start coming in. Most financial counselors recommend that you stop charging when your credit payments (not including a mortgage) approach 15 to 20 percent of your take-home pay. To determine whether you owe too much, check the following warning signs:

Kill the Cards

Take steps now, before you retire, to get off the cards. How do you go about killing a credit card? You simply take it out of your wallet or purse and cut it up into small pieces. Wonderful things will happen to you once you kick the credit card habit. You'll start buying less of what you really don't need. Each card has a limit to the amount of credit you can get. If you have many credit accounts, the total limit available to you may be more than you can handle. So it's really up to you to establish the credit limit that you can realistically handle. The first step is to determine what your personal credit limit should be by figuring out how much you can afford to pay each month for credit purchases. Once you establish your personal credit limit, plan your credit spending so that your total payments cover, at a minimum, your credit purchases plus interest.

Limit yourself to one or two cards. You should consider keeping cards that are widely accepted throughout the world, and keep the ones with the best interest rates. Next, record everything you charge in a memo book so you know where you are at any time during the month. You may be able to do this step online by viewing your account activities on your card's website. This will eliminate surprises at the end of the month when you get your bill and exclaim, "Wow, I didn't realize I spent that much." If you are truly in debt with your cards, and struggle not to use them, then you may have to get rid of your cards altogether. Depending on your situation, you may want to look into getting a consolidation loan to pay them off.

Several different kinds of credit cards are available to the general public. Some have lower interest rates, but you pay an annual fee. Other varieties offer competitive interest rates, but vary in their features. The best way to find out all the options and choose the best one for you is at *www.e-wisdom.com*. This site offers personalized recommendations, based on information you supply, and shows comparison charts so that you can see the differences between all the cards offered. You may also choose to look at *www.cardratings.com,* which offers a variety of resources to help you understand everything related to credit cards.

If You Have to Borrow

The best way to borrow money is through whatever means is available to you that offers the lowest interest rate possible. Do your research to find the best rate available. Depending on the amount of money you need, you can look at the low interest incentives offered through your current credit card or home equity line of credit.

There are several good ways to pay for big-ticket items. Cash is preferred. If you can't pay for something with cash, you should reconsider whether you really need this item. If you use your credit card, it should only be because you are in a situation where you can't use cash, and you know that you will be able to pay-off the bill in full at the end of the month, before interest starts accruing. Another option is to borrow money. However, borrowed money typically comes with a price. Generally this is in the form of an interest rate, so to be careful of the rate offered you and know how it works. For example, if you decide to buy a new car, there may be several car companies that offer low interest rates to buyers. Just make sure you read the fine print in any deal that you sign up for.

Watch Out for Your Car

According to the U.S. Department of Transportation, the total cost of driving a car 25,000 miles annually is $7,500, or about 30 cents a mile. Car payments are not included in their calculation, but depreciation is a big part of the number. For example, if you purchase a new car for $25,000, it's estimated that your car instantly depreciates by about $5,000 as soon as you drive it off the car lot. Before you set out to buy a car, decide what kind of vehicle you need and what options are necessary. Consider fuel efficiency, seating capacity, overall size, your use of this car, and so on. Once you have your list, begin your research. For a comprehensive car-buying guide, go to *www.intellichoice.com* or *www.edmunds.com*.

Some people think that leasing is not substantially different than financing a car, and because monthly lease payments are typically lower than what it costs to finance a car, they assume that leasing is the less expensive option. However, that may not be the case. Leasing a vehicle is very different from buying one. When you lease, you are, in effect, renting a car for a specified period of time. Because you don't own it, you are obligated, under a lease contract, to maintain the vehicle and drive it a limited number of miles per year. If you try to get out of a lease before it expires, you will be required to pay significant penalty costs. Take a moment to answer the following questions to determine whether leasing is a viable option for you:

1. Do you typically trade in a new car every four years or less?

2. Do you, on average, drive fewer than 15,000 miles a year?

3. Do you need a new car every few years for whatever reason?

If you answered "yes" to one or more of these questions, then you might want to consider leasing. Shop around and get lease contract details and bids from at least two dealers on the vehicle you want.

Over a five-year period, a new car will depreciate an estimated 30 to 50 percent. Most of the depreciation occurs within the first two years. Therefore, an advantage is to consider buying a used vehicle that's three or four years old. That way, you are not experiencing the depreciation and actually benefit from someone else's loss. A good way to determine how much the car you are considering depreciates is to go to *www.edmunds.com*. Review what the new cost of the model would be versus what value it holds after two, three, or four years. This may help you decide whether you would like to buy this car new or used.

Create a Retirement Plan

A retirement plan is your yellow brick road to retirement land. If you follow it, it will get you there. To begin your plan, you need to find a helpful tool to use. There are literally hundreds of websites that have been created to assist boomers in all aspects of retirement planning. Some offer specific retirement advice or special services, while others offer information exchanges between yourself and others. We've listed several of the better sites in our Appendix A to give you an idea of what's out there and to assist you in your retirement planning efforts. One particular favorite is Fidelity Investment's website (fidelity.com) because it offers several services that are available to individuals.

You may ask the question, based on your age, how should you structure your retirement plan? The best way to answer this question is to have you go through the process of creating a plan based on where you are right now and where you hope to be at retirement. However, if you would like to get some preliminary information, you can do a quick fifteen minute retirement plan review by going to *www.money.cnn.com* and searching for the *Money* magazine article, "The 15 Minute Retirement Plan."

We can't repeat it enough. To be successful, you have to have a well thought out retirement plan in place. We've outlined six steps that people who have successfully retired took to ensure the financial success of their retirement:

Diversification Strategy. Before you invest in anything, decide how you want to diversify your portfolio. Your diversification plan should be in place before you make your first investment. Learn all you can by reading and studying everything you can get your hands on about investing. Learn about short-term and long-term investment options so that you can decide which investments are best for you.

Emergency Fund in Place. Create an emergency fund. Unexpected expenses can include uninsured medical costs, auto repairs, and unemployment. Your goal here may be to pay all your monthly bills without relying on future cash sources such as bonuses or credit to cover routine expenses. Make sure you have insurance to cover disability, health, life, automobiles, and your personal property.

Credit Cards Under Control. Be careful with how you use your credit cards. If you use credit cards to pay for everything and struggle to pay the monthly balance off, then you have a challenge. Consider changing your spending habits so that you can pay off high-interest credit cards each month before you begin investing.

Well Managed Retirement Accounts. If you have retirement accounts such as IRAs, make sure you're making full independent contributions to these accounts before you start investing in anything else. If you have a pension plan in place with your current employer, make sure you know exactly what it will be worth before you retire. For example, if you have determined that you'll need $50,000 of income a year to retire, and you feel confident that you can, on average, earn 10 percent on your investments, then you'll need $500,000 in your retirement account.

Own a Home. If you don't own a home, buy one. It is one of the best tax shelters you can get, and unless you are in a depressed area of the country, you should enjoy appreciation on just about any home you buy, particularly if you are willing to buy in a low market and wait to sell until the market is in an upswing. The other thing to consider when purchasing a home is to buy the lowest priced home in the neighborhood. This can yield the highest appreciation for the owner and all the expenditures in necessary repairs, maintenance, and upkeep will render more profit to you in the end because you have more potential for appreciation.

Maximizing Retirement Accounts. Max out your retirement savings. With most of your major expenses hopefully behind you, it's time to push the savings throttle down and maximize your allowable contributions in your retirement plans (401(k), IRA, etc.). If you are 50-plus, you can start taking advantage of what is called catch-up contributions, which allow you to contribute an extra $5,000 in your 401(k) and an extra $1,000 in a Roth IRA. That's a total of $20,000 through your employee 401(k) contribution of $15,000 and an additional $5,000 for your catch-up contribution. You can also have up to $5,000 for a Roth IRA.

Finding Extra Money. Organize your outstanding loans from the highest to the lowest interest rates. If possible, increase the amount of your payments against your high interest loans first to get them paid off. Consider refinancing if it can be done at a lower interest rate than the interest rates on your other debts. Use the money you save to pay off existing debts. If you pay a $20 monthly minimum on a $1,000 credit card that charges 18 percent interest, it'll take you ninety-four months to pay the loan off If you increased the payments to $40 a month, you'll pay the loan off in just thirty four months and can use the extra money for savings.

Extra work. Consider doing work on the side and put the money you earn into savings. This will expedite your efforts in reaching your financial retirement goals.

You don't want to learn the hard way and find financial holes in your plan once you're into your retirement. If you are not 150 percent confident that the final written plan will work, then don't do it. It's okay to include contingency plans in your master retirement plan if certain assumptions that you have made don't work out. In fact, if you don't have lots of contingencies built into your plan, you probably don't have a solid plan.

Chapter 2

Manage Your Money

Ben Franklin once said if you save enough nickels,
they will add up to a dollar some day

There's no question that the biggest fear for people when it comes to retirement is financial. Will they have enough money to support themselves and their dependents throughout their retirement years? According to *Forbes* magazine, most people fail to meet their monthly expenses *within the first year* after they retire. Many retirees fail because they didn't have plans or specific goals before they retired. Be careful not to fall into that same trap. You can head off the biggest fear by saving enough money to retire comfortably. We'll show you ways to do that in this chapter.

Retirement Accounts Are Critical

Most retirement accounts fall into one of two categories: defined benefit or defined contribution accounts. In a defined benefit account, the employer commits to the benefit and takes on the responsibility of managing the account. The benefit is based on what's in the plan when you retire. For example, an employer may define an account that requires the company to deposit a fixed annual sum of money into the account for each eligible employee (i.e., a defined benefit).

When an employee retires, they are then entitled to the money that the employer deposited on her behalf. Defined contribution accounts outline what the employer's contribution will be. The accounts are usually profit-sharing and/or salary reduction plans. Profit-sharing plans pay into the plan based on a percentage of profits earned by the company. Obviously, there are no guarantees and if there are no profits, nothing gets deposited into the account.

Defined contribution accounts allow employees to set aside income on a pretax basis, such as into a 401(k) account. Employers can commit to match all or part of an employee's contribution into the account. Defined contribution accounts shift all retirement risks onto the employee. What they accumulate in their account depends on how much was contributed and how the funds were invested. The retirement accounts below outlines the different options.

401(k) accounts are available to employees working for profit businesses. Every employee qualifies for up to 15% of their salary or $9,500, whichever is less

403(b) accounts are available to employees working for nonprofit businesses. Every employee qualifies for up to 20% of their salary or $9,500, whichever is less.

IRAs are available to anyone with earned income. Up to $5,000 earned income can be deposited tax free annually depending on your age.

How can you find out if your pension plan and private retirement accounts are secure? To determine whether your plan is safe, consider working with a financial professional and have him go over your plan with you. For a fee, he will make sure that your plan is diverse and that your investments are fairly safe depending on your age, your retirement goals, and the financial stability of the company you work for. For example, if you are getting close to retirement, a financial expert would most likely look for low-risk investments in your retirement accounts. If you are younger and are comfortable with taking risks, he might suggest adding more aggressive investments to your accounts. Having an analysis done on your pension fund will give you peace of mind so that you can sleep at night and be assured that your retirement planning is still on track.

As you get closer to retirement, start shifting your priorities from wealth-building investments to "making it last" investments. Investments that can produce a steady stream of income will become critical in your retirement years. Bonds are one way to add income at a low risk. T. Rowe Price (800-638-5660) is one of many sources that offer high-quality tax free municipal bonds that you can buy. Another alternative is to invest in high-dividend blue-chip stocks.

For example, J.P. Morgan Chase (stock exchange symbol JPM) is an internationally recognized bank that pays 3 percent annual dividends on its stock. Make sure you have the time and inclination to research and track any stock you buy, as well as the fortitude to withstand the ups and downs of the stock market. For those who are not interested in tracking the stock market on a regular basis, check out T Rowe Price's retirement mutual funds (800-638-5660). Their retirement funds invest in a mix of stocks and bonds that get more conservative as you get older. Fidelity's balanced fund works the same way (800-343-3548).

Using Rollovers

A rollover is a procedure that the IRS designed that allows you to roll over assets from one retirement plan into another. For example, if you change jobs or retire, you can transfer assets from one retirement account to another-such as from an employer sponsored 401(k) plan into an IRA protecting your tax-free status and avoiding any early-withdrawal penalties. There are several advantages to rolling over your managed IRA plans into a self-directed plan. Self-directed IRAs offer you a range of investment choices such as mutual funds, stocks, bonds, and CDs that are not traditionally offered by managed plans.

Minimizing Taxes

You've heard it before. There are two sure things in this world that are certain - death and taxes. It is estimated that Americans spend over a billion hours each year preparing their tax returns. Given that amount of time and effort spent on this dreaded task, it is no wonder that the subject of taxes creates a lot of emotion and misconceptions. As a result, many people make poor decisions when it comes to dealing with their taxes. They wonder: Should I prepare my own tax return? How do the tax laws affect my retirement accounts? How do I minimize my tax liabilities after I retire? Although the entire topic of taxes can't be covered in a single chapter-or in an entire book, for that matter-we do address major tax issues that you should be aware of before and after you retire.

In 1997 Congress passed an IRS reform bill, which makes it much easier for the average taxpayer to receive fair treatment under the tax laws. Under the law, known as the Tax Relief Act of 1997, the burden of tax-fraud proof is the responsibility of the government instead of the taxpayer. Prior to this law, mistreated taxpayers could not sue the IRS for damages. Now, with the passing of the law, they can. The law expanded eligibility for traditional IRAs and created the Roth IRA and new education IRAs to help pay college expenses for your children. The Roth IRA is a variation of the traditional IRA. While maximum contribution levels to a Roth IRA are the same as for a regular IRA (i.e., $4,000 or $5,000 per person per year depending on age), tax treatment and eligibility are much different. Your contributions to a Roth are not tax-deductible, but your withdrawals are tax-free as long as the account has been open at least five years and the withdrawals are made after age 591/2.

Your income level is the sole determining factor for Roth IRA eligibility. To contribute the full amount per year per individual, your adjusted gross income must be $99,000 or less for single taxpayers and $156,000 or less for joint filers (in 2007). The new Roth option can give you a reason to re-evaluate your retirement strategy. Is it better to pay taxes now and avoid paying them later or is it better to defer taxes now? The answer depends on your present and future financial situation.

Preparing Your Tax Return

People probably experience more anxiety about taxes than they do about any other financial planning issue. However, as you move closer toward retirement, your taxes will, in all will probability be considerably less than they were during your working years. In this chapter, we will address questions and answers that will help you minimize the turmoil that is often associated with taxes.

You might opt to use an accountant over doing their own taxes for several reasons. You may feel more comfortable having a professional reviewing your taxes. Another reason is to utilize the professional's expertise in hopes of finding potential tax breaks and cost-saving strategies based on your personal situation. Finally, if you have a more complex tax return, you may prefer having accountants do the job. It will cost you money to use an accountant, and you have to decide if you would feel more comfortable using an accountant or if you are fine with doing it yourself.

A top-notch tax accountant can save you a lot of aggravation preparing your tax return, and in many cases, identify deductions that you have overlooked. The type of tax accountant you need will depend on the complexity of your return, where you are in your financial plan, and how much you're willing to pay. You basically have three options to consider:

Storefront tax preparers. These are the people who work for companies such as H&R Block that maintain storefronts in mini-malls throughout the country. Most of these people are working part-time during the tax season and have been trained to ask you the right questions and fill out tax returns. They generally have a limited background in tax accounting, so do not expect them to offer you any strategic advice, which is a disadvantage of using storefront tax preparers.

Accountants. Accountants, by our definition, are people who have a minimum of four-year college degrees in accounting. Most of them work as accountants for companies and moonlight out of their homes to earn extra money during the tax season. They have an edge over storefront tax preparers since they have accounting degrees and work full-time in the accounting field.

Certified Public Accountants (CPAs). CPAs are considered the tax professionals of the industry. If you have a complex return, need tough questions answered on your current return, require year-round tax and investment-planning advice, and help just in case you're audited by the IRS, then you need a CPA. And yes, they are the most expensive route to go.

Be Prepared

To get the most benefit out of a tax professional, always arrive prepared when you meet with your tax professional. Most of them charge for their services on an hourly basis, so if you waste their time because you're not prepared, you'll pay for it. If you are meeting with one for tax and investment-planning advice, be prepared to tell him what you want to do in the current year and what your forecasted plans are for the next three to five years. Write your plans down in outline form so he won't have to take notes, which again takes time and costs you money. Don't assume that your tax preparer is an expert in everything that's important to you. Do your own research and homework so that you can carry on an informed conversation about key topics.

Also, keep your tax preparer informed about any changes in your family situation that could affect your tax status, such as a divorce, a new baby, or a marriage. If you are considering taking a tax deduction that you think is legally borderline, give him all the facts and ask for his opinion about the risk of an audit. In other words, treat your tax professional as a strategic partner who is interested in helping you achieve your financial goals.

After your return has been prepared by a tax-return professional, ask her what you can do to reduce your taxes next year. This may require a follow-up visit with your accountant after the tax season is over. Or, if you are using a seasonal accountant, ask for her advice at the same time you're having your return prepared. You may want to meet again with your tax preparer in November or December if you are considering dumping some stock and taking the loss, or, on the upside, selling and taking the capital gain hit. You may have some last-minute decisions to make on IRA or 401(k) investments to improve your overall tax situation.

How long do you need to keep my tax returns and records? According to the IRS, "you must keep your records as long as they may be needed for the administration of any provision of the Internal Revenue Code." Generally, this means you must keep records that support items on your return until the period of

limitations for that return runs out (see their website at
www.irs.gov). In most cases, you are required to keep your tax
return and backup records for three years. If you think the IRS may
have questions regarding your income reporting, then keep records
for six years or longer. Keep all employment tax records for at least
four years after the date that the tax becomes due or is paid,
whichever is later.

Preparing Your Own Tax Return

You can save time and money by doing your own taxes. Consider
using some of the great tax-preparation software on the market that
will walk you through the process. Tax-preparation software is, in
our opinion, one of the best applications ever created for the
personal computer. It virtually does away with tedious calculations,
helps eliminate math errors, and automatically produces the tax
forms you need to complete your return. That last feature in and of
itself makes the software purchase worthwhile.

Most of the user-friendly tax software walks you through a series of
questions about your tax return and calculates the final information
based upon your responses to the questions. When you are done, the
application provides you with official, completed tax return forms
that are ready for submission. It will even ask you if you want it to
file your return electronically, which expedites the process. And you
get all this for about $30 to $50 for the federal tax software and
about $10 for your state tax software. It's an amazing deal when you
think about it. One of the better software applications available is
TurboTax by Intuit Corporation. You can get more information and
compare their tax products on their website at
www.turbotax.intuit.com.

Property Taxes

In the past five years, property taxes have risen 40 percent. Property
taxes will keep rising nearly everywhere for homeowners even as
house prices are falling in many parts of the country, according to a
USA Today analysis of government data. Unfortunately, the quality
of public education, which property taxes largely supports, has gone

downhill in many sections of the country. In recent years, states such as Colorado and Oregon have been swept by anti-property tax groups that have managed to force tax levies back through the legislative process. There are several things you can do to lower your property taxes. Find out if you qualify for any special property tax exemptions in your state. For obvious reasons, most states don't publicize these. However, many states offer exemptions if you're older than 65, disabled, a veteran, or in other special group classifications.

Check the accuracy of your home's assessed value by reviewing the property record card that is on file at your assessor's office. Most of the cards are now on a computer file. The card lists all of the features of your property upon which your tax is based, such as lot size, square footage, and improvements. If your home's features are overstated, you could be paying more taxes than you should, and you could refute the value to lower the taxes through the assessor's office.

If you believe your home is assessed too high, document your case before you see the tax assessor. If part of your case is based on the value of comparable properties in your neighborhood, you'll need written verification of three to five comparable homes. Photographs will help strengthen your case, so include those with your documents. Make sure you follow the appeal process of your county's government to the letter. Be unfailingly courteous whenever you talk to county officials. Anger won't cut it if you're trying to solicit their cooperation. If the county appeals board rejects your challenge, you can challenge the board in court at the state level or file your complaint with the state review board. That can be an expensive proposition and will probably require an attorney, so make sure it will be worth your time and money.

Chapter 3

Money Making Strategies

If you plan to live forever, make sure you invest enough money to cover yourself!

If you want your hard-earned money to continue to grow and prosper after you retire, you need to begin building an investment portfolio that encompasses your goals, risk tolerance, and time horizon. Your ultimate financial goal may be to retire in style. How soon you retire, and in what style, can significantly affect your decisions on how you invest your money in stocks, bonds, and mutual funds.

Investment Strategies

Should you buy a mutual fund or that hot stock that your golf buddy told you about? How do you choose between stocks and bonds? Should you look into investing in real estate or starting a personal business? There are logical answers to these questions. Start with a sensible investment plan. *Money* magazine's website has a feature that is called Money 10l at www.*money.cnn.com* that walks you through the basics of investment types and what you need to know. Stocks, bonds and funds are just a few of the types of investments that are covered.

This site is a great place to start to understand your different investment options and what to look out for. You will need to review each investment option in detail to help you determine the right strategy for you. Here's an overview of important investment issues you should consider to make money:

Is time on your side? Investors with more years until retirement can afford to put a greater percentage of their assets in the stock market. If time is not on your side, you may want to consider conservative mutual funds or bonds.

Stocks mean risk with higher returns. Investors with a higher tolerance for volatility should put more money in the stock market than those who have a lower tolerance for risk. Get professional advice. One of the best ways to build a solid portfolio is to periodically consult a qualified broker or knowledgeable friend for advice and ideas.

Make diversification a key goal. Studies show that asset diversification is the single most important factor in determining solid returns from both short- and long-term investments.

As a rule of thumb, revise your investment plan as soon as things change (the economy, your personal life, etc.). In fact, if you don't do it at least once every six months, you are probably not monitoring your investments as you should. Diversify your portfolio across different industries and sectors. For example, you may decide to invest in five to ten stocks from different industries and never let anyone be more than 20 percent of your total portfolio. If there is a sudden downturn in the economy, it may be appropriate to pull your money out of the market and put it into a money market account until things get better.

Opening a Brokerage Account

Stock brokerage firms are basically cash-and-carry enterprises. They all require client prospects to submit an application and a minimum specified amount to open an account before you can start trading. When you place an order, your broker withdraws money from your cash account to cover the trade. If you sell stock or receive a dividend, the broker adds that money to your cash account. If you develop a good history, your broker may allow you to place trades without funds in your cash account if you settle the deficit within a few days. However, be aware that nearly all brokerages include disclaimers in their application forms that make you responsible for whatever you instruct them to do on your behalf, whether verbally or in writing.

Commission structures change radically between brokerage firms, depending on the wide variety of special features they may offer. When deciding which broker is best for you, factor in the features that are important to you. Here's how to find a good broker:

Conduct interviews with brokers that interest you. Make sure you are providing them with accurate information on your investment goals so that you get the best recommendations for your needs.

Get references. During the personal interview, ask for names of satisfied clients they have worked with over the past two years. Talk to other clients of the brokerage. If the brokerage has no references for you, then you may have uncovered a problem. If a broker has many highly satisfied clients, then at least one of them should be willing to talk to you on the brokerage's behalf. Also, don't hesitate to ask for your broker's credentials.

Know what they charge. Make sure you understand and are comfortable with your broker's commission structure, any annual fees, transaction costs, and any other expenses that you could incur. Find out what "free" information the brokerage firm will send you such as research reports, company announcements, and annual reports.

If all of this sounds like a huge time investment, you're correct. A good broker can make you financially independent. Conversely, a bad one can cause you a lot of financial damage.

Trading Online

In Burton Malkiel's classic book, *A Random Walk Down Wall Street,* he debunks virtually every popular theory of stock selection employed by the gurus of Wall Street. Malkiel and his dart throwing chimp theory caused much controversy. He contended that a blindfolded chimpanzee throwing darts at the *Wall Street Journal* stock page could select a portfolio that would do as well as one carefully selected by the Wall Street experts. Needless to say, Malkiel was not very popular on Wall Street. A successful stockbroker has a hundred or more clients. If that broker was to call each of their clients during the trading day and you were one of them, they would only have a couple of minutes to devote to you. If the market is in a sudden downturn or upturn, your chances of getting through to your broker are next to impossible.

As an alternative, if you log onto an online broker site, you can instantly see what's happening in the market, enter buy or sell orders, track your portfolio, transfer funds, and conduct investment research, all with the click of a mouse button. While full-service brokers charge up to a $250 commission fee per trade, an online broker's commission can be as low as $8 for the same trade. That's a whopping 350 percent savings on commission fees. Although online brokers don't offer as many of the personal services as full-service brokers, most do offer online research tools to help you get whatever information you might need to make intelligent investment decisions.

Word of mouth counts for a lot when it comes to selecting an online brokerage firm. Ask your friends who are actively trading stocks which firm they're using and if they like them. Also, when considering an online broker, it's important to look beyond commissions. Check for hidden fees. Some online brokers charge a start-up fee to open an account, or an administrative charge per trade.

Do they have a website that works for you? A well-organized trading and research screen with safeguards built in to guard against data entry errors is a must. Do you have access to real-time quotes (i.e., are stock prices current when displayed)? Some brokers provide quotes that are delayed as much as 15 minutes unless you pay extra for real-time quotes.

Create a Watch List

A watch list is a listing of stocks and mutual funds that are, for whatever reason, of interest to you. A typical watch list includes the name and trade symbol of the equity you're "watching," the share price on the day you incorporated it into your list, and a brief reason why you added it to your list (e.g., recommendation from friend, magazine article, etc.). The purpose of the list is to watch specific stocks or funds over some period of time to determine how they perform in the market, before you invest in them.

Almost every broker organization, as well as many online brokers offer their clients the option to create a watch list online through their websites. This list is a way for you to monitor potential investments and personalize it based on your investments strategies. You can create a watch list manually on a piece of paper if you don't have access to one on the Internet. Either way, it is an effective way to monitor your investments.

It is highly recommended that you follow funds that you are potentially interested in buying on your watch list. Enter the per-share price as of the date you added it to your watch list. Over time, does it appreciate to your satisfaction? Follow the returns of any fund that you invest in by using the same price-monitoring techniques that you did on your watch list. Put funds on your watch list and portfolio just as you would with stocks. It's an easy way to keep an eye on a fund and stay engaged with your mutual fund investments.

Your Portfolio

Similar to a watch list, a portfolio is a listing of stocks and mutual funds that you actually own. A typical portfolio includes the name and trade symbol of the equity you own, the number of shares, the price per share that you paid on the day you incorporated it into your portfolio, and a brief reason why you bought it. The purpose of a portfolio is to help you track the performance of stocks or funds you own to determine how they are performing in the market.

A portfolio is usually setup online so it can be updated easily. Every major brokerage organization, including Internet brokers, offers their clients the option to create a portfolio online using their websites. Many offer this feature as part of their customer service. You can reference *www.ehow.com* to get a simple list of things you need to do in order to set up and use a portfolio.

Some of the top financial information sources that are easy to navigate are:

Charles Schwab at *www.schwab.com*

Investor's Business Daily at *www.investors.com*

Money magazine at *www.money.cnn.com*

Yahoo Financial at *wwwjinance.yahoo.com*

Financial News at *wwwjinancialnews-us.com*

To establish your goals and objectives for any investment planning, you will need to conduct a financial analysis of your current investment positions. If you have already done this, then you are off to a good start. Your goals should include preservation and appreciation of principle and the generation of a stable after-tax income. Your objectives will be derived from your goals and will help you to determine your future financial state based on your desired standard of living.

Stop Loss Strategy

There are ways to defend your portfolio against major losses. There is a stock sell feature that is worth reviewing; it is called a stop loss. What this allows you to do is to put in a sell order if the stock you purchased drops to a certain price. Generally speaking, you typically would consider a stop loss of 10 percent less than your purchase price. For example, if you buy a stock at $100 a share, you may want to subsequently put in a stop loss order through your broker for $90. This means that if the stock you purchased goes down to $90, you are putting in the order to have the stock sold for you. You would experience a loss of $10 a share, but you are also protecting yourself against a major loss so that if it drops dramatically (i.e., more than 10 percent), you did not absorb additional losses on the stock. A stop loss also gives you the freedom of not having to monitor a stock as closely as you would without it because the sell is automated. For additional information about the stop loss feature, go to *www.schwab.com* and search for stop loss.

Diversification Strategy

Before you start investing in anything, make sure you know how diversified you want to be in your investment portfolio. This is important because diversifying your accounts keeps your portfolio in balance. Many boomers may not know if their investments are diversified because the mutual funds and stocks that they own are in their retirement accounts. If this applies to you, find out exactly what you plan to invest in. For example, some funds call themselves small cap. But, given the less-than-stellar performance of large-cap stocks over the past few years, these same funds may have veered off into small-cap territory to boost their returns. It's your duty to understand where your money is invested, so make sure you get this information and review it. Without this knowledge, you could be under the false assumption that your stocks are diversified across companies. Consider using dollar cost averaging to help you diversify. Dollar cost averaging is a strategy of buying securities (typically mutual funds and stocks) in fixed dollar amounts at scheduled intervals, with the aim being to lower the average cost per share over time.

How Many Equities Should You Own?

There is no right or wrong answer as to how many equities (i.e., stocks, bonds, funds, etc.) you should own in your investment program. However, you want to make sure your portfolio is diversified, and we caution you against investing all of your money into stocks alone. With this in mind, you can get a better idea of the amount of stock you should own once you determine your investment strategy and develop your watch list. You also want to make sure that your portfolio is manageable for you, so limit the amount of stocks, bonds and funds you own based on your comfort level.

Don't chase hot trends. Be skeptical of a friend's advice when his recommendation does not include specific information as to why you should buy the stock. This sort of buying behavior is extremely risky. Many of us saw a number of high-tech stocks that were trading at price earnings (PE) ratios in excess of 100 in the late 1990s go on to crash in 2000. Exorbitantly high PEs of certain stocks in the late 1990s led to the meltdown of the market in early 2000 through 2003. Most astute stock investors will tell you that they avoid stocks with PEs that are greater than 20.

Develop your own strategies and your own system for following potentially attractive stocks. In the end, there is one fact on which all the experts agree: over time, the price of quality stocks always moves up. A good reference to review and analyze stock is *www.stat-usa.gov.This* site is sponsored by the U.S. Department of Commerce and provides financial information, economic news, indicators, and statistics that affect stocks.

Saving Strategies

The typical rule of thumb is to save at least 10 percent of your salary. If you can afford to save at least this amount, then you're doing great. If you are following this model, you should be on track for a healthy savings toward your retirement. A good retirement plan separates savings into three categories or funds for different purposes: an emergency savings fund, a short-term savings fund, and a long-term savings fund. The emergency fund is the most important savings category. It is created to cover income and expenses related to emergencies such as the loss of a job or unexpected medical expenses.

Most financial planners will advise you to accumulate six months of income in your emergency fund. The funds should be kept in an easy-to-access account with no penalty for withdrawal. Short-term savings funds are used for planned expenses such as a vacation or major purchases such as a car or furniture. Regular recurring contributions are essential to assure that your "nest egg" builds at a consistent rate.

Long-term funds are typically invested in equities that can provide long-term growth. Building equity in your home is a powerful way to grow your long-term savings account. Aggressive mortgage payments handled either by increasing the amount of your monthly payment or by making extra payments, are two popular ways to increase the equity in your home and expedite paying off your house.

Compound Interest Strategy

You hear a lot about using compound interest to accumulate retirement funds. What is it?
Compound interest is the interest paid and accumulated on dollars that are invested at a fixed rate of return. As a saver, understand how compound interest works and how to use it to get ahead financially. The compound interest "rule of 72" dramatically illustrates how compound interest works. Divide 72 by the yield you expect to make on a given investment. The result is how long it will take to double your money. For example, if you estimate that an investment you own will yield 18 percent annually, then you will double your money in four years ($72/18 = 4$).

So when interest is added to the account balance, the interest earned on the investment earns additional interest during the duration of the investment. This compounding rate is what we classify as compound interest. You may have heard that using compound interest is beneficial for retirement because there are some advantages for savers who choose to use compound interest in their favor. To read and understand this in greater detail, visit *www.banking.about.com* and do a search on compound interest.

Chapter 4

Investing In Stocks, Bonds & Funds

The secret to smart investing is to keep it simple stupid

Stocks, bonds and funds can offer you advantageous investment opportunities, but they have some red flags that you should be aware of. In difficult bear markets, bonds can provide the ballast in your portfolio. However, bonds typically generate a slower rate of return than stocks and funds. Although stock and funds can provide you a higher rate of return on your money, you are more susceptible to volatile and uncontrollable influences on the market. Ultimately, balancing your portfolio with stocks, bonds and funds is a solid strategy to provide the diversity that you need.

Risk Tolerance

Risk tolerance is a means for measuring your individualized willingness to take investment risks in exchange for a higher potential for return on your money. To measure the level of risk you are willing to take, it is important to understand how aggressive an investor you truly are. To determine this, you can take a risk tolerance test by going to *http://money.aol.com/investing*, going to Investing Basics, and clicking "What Kind of Investor Are You? Take the Quiz."

If you have a high tolerance for volatility, you may want to invest as much as 70 percent of your holdings in the stock market, 25 percent in bonds, and only 5 percent in a money market account. If you have less stomach for volatility, you may want to keep 50 percent in stocks or mutual funds, 40 percent in bonds, and the rest in money market accounts.

Investing in Stocks

Over the long term, stocks can be an extremely profitable investment. Stocks offer you two key benefits as an investment. The first is real growth. Historically speaking, stocks have run 7 percentage points over inflation and generally yield a healthier return on your money than other investment opportunities.

The percentage of ownership you have in the company is in direct proportion to the quantity of shares that you purchase. For example, if a company has 10,000 outstanding shares and you purchase 1,000 shares of stock, you own 10 percent of that company. Most stocks also offer voting rights to their owners, which provides shareholders with a proportional vote at annual stockholders' meetings.

Stock offers the opportunity for individuals to take part in the ownership of a corporation in hopes of gaining equity as the stock value increases. As we have seen, many people have done extremely well in the stock market, but other individuals have lost a fortune. For example, many have enjoyed the ride with Microsoft, while others took the loss experienced with Enron. The market is volatile, and investing in stock can be lucrative if done with caution. It can make your retirement, but if you're not careful, it can break it as well.

If you're considering buying stock in one of two companies where one pays dividends and the other doesn't, then buy the one with dividends if everything else in your comparison analysis is the same. Dividends are cash returns paid out to stockholders at a predetermined time, typically annually or semiannually, as a return on their investment in the company's stock. Dividend payouts are also subject to being taxed.

Companies that don't pay dividends simply reinvest what they would have paid in dividends back into the company. Some investment analysts would argue that dividends are bad because the companies that issue them "probably" don't have anything better to do with their capital. Others assert that recognizing stockholders and meeting business needs is a sign of good management. Dividends are also a sign of profitability, since they're paid out of the profits the company makes. Companies that are losing money will tell you that dividends aren't important. Ask their public relations officer where they're investing their cash. They probably don't know.

Investing in Bonds

Basically, a bond is an agreement between the bond issuer, who is borrowing the money, and the bondholder, who is lending the money. Each bond agreement is characterized by two primary questions: How long does the bond issuer (borrower) have to repay the bondholder (lender or you)? What interest rates will the issuer pay and when will interest payments be made?

Bonds offer you an alternative investment to stocks and funds. If the bears are racing through the stock market, bonds can offer you a safe haven to park your money until things get better. In difficult bear markets, bonds can provide the ballast in your portfolio to offset losses in the stock market. The financial strength of the issuer of a bond is a key factor in your decision to invest in a bond. Obviously, if you're lending money, the first thing you want to know is the borrower's ability to pay back your principle plus interest based on the borrower's credit history. In addition to its financial strength, the duration of the bond is critical. Usually, the more time the issuer has to repay, the higher the interest rate.

There are several options in the bond market. General obligation bonds are backed by the full taxing power of the local or state government issuing the bonds. Limited tax bonds are secured by a pledge from a specific tax or category of taxes, such as a cigarette or gasoline tax. Revenue bonds are issued to finance facilities that are expected to be self-supporting, such as toll roads and baseball parks. Historically, state and municipal bonds have had an excellent performance record for paying out interest and principle. Even during the Great Depression of the 1930s, 98 percent of all municipalities met their bond obligations. In many cases, you can buy bonds directly from the issuing government agency to avoid stockbroker commissions. Here is a summary of what is available in the bond market:

U.S. Treasuries are issued by the U.S. government. Treasury bonds consist of Treasury bills that mature in 13 weeks to one year. Treasury bonds mature in 10 or more years.

Risk: Considered one of the safest bonds, guaranteed by the U.S. government.

Taxes: State and local taxes tax-free but subject to federal taxes.

Mortgage-Backed Bonds are made up of a pool on individual mortgages bundled together by the Government National Mortgage Association (Genie Mae), Federal home Loan Mortgage Corporation (Freddie Mac), or Federal National Mortgage Association (Fannie Mae).

Risk: Only Genie Mae are guaranteed and backed by the U.S. government.

Taxes: Interest is taxable.

Corporate Bonds are issued by corporations usually in $1,000 increments and have maturities ranging from a few weeks up to 100 years.

Risk: An investment-grade bond is relatively safe and has a high bond rating.

Taxes: Taxes: Interest is taxable.

Municipal Bonds are issued by states, cities, and local government agencies and institutions to raise money for government developed facilities.

Risk: Generally lower risk with lower yields than most other bonds.

Taxes: Federal-tax-free along with most state and local taxes.

To boost bond sales, the Treasury Department is now selling inflation-indexed savings bonds, which are also known as I bonds. All I bonds' interest rates are based on the consumer price index, and you can earn interest for up to thirty years. The earnings for I bonds fluctuate with the economy; generally, they will increase in value on a monthly basis. You can buy ten and thirty year inflation indexed Treasury bonds that guarantee a return that will outpace inflation. When inflation rates are low, Treasury bond payout is unlikely to beat regular savings bonds. But if inflation heats up, so will the bonds' appeal, and their interest rates will proportionately meet and even exceed the inflation rate. If you would like to learn more about this topic, consider reading the free resource called *The Savings Bonds Question and Answer Book* that's published by the Department of the Treasury, U.S. Savings Bonds Marketing Department, Washington DC 20226.

An important factor to note about owning bonds is the standard interest rate (i.e., prime rate) that's available in the market at any given time. If the market interest rate falls, bond prices usually move higher, because the interest they are paying is worth more when compared to current lower rates. When interest rates move higher, bond prices tend to move lower. For additional information on how to benefit from investing in bonds, go to the Bond Market Association's website at *www.investinginbonds.com*. If you're just starting out investing in bonds, this site will help you learn more about bonds or investment strategies.

Investing in Mutual Funds

The secret to investing in mutual funds is simplicity. Wall Street is constantly urging buyers to purchase this and buy that. However, chances are that the more complicated the fund is, the riskier it is. "Flashy" funds almost always profit the vendors selling them more than they profit you. You don't need to own complicated funds. You can rack up a superb retirement nest egg with just three or four good stocks or bonds owning mutual funds.

A mutual fund is an open-ended investment operated by an investment company that raises money from shareholders and invests in one lump investment (i.e., the fund) that typically has a common investment objective. The investment objectives between funds can vary widely, with some investing in small-cap companies and others in large-cap companies. Mutual funds offer investors the opportunity to pool their money together and buy into multiple stocks, bonds, and real estate. Choosing the right mutual funds offers a way for you to diversify your investments and reap the benefits of a nice return on your money.

Most funds offer the benefit of allowing you to deposit a certain amount each month into the fund to increase the number of shares you own. By spreading your investment out over time, you develop a consistent savings plan within your investment plan. Here are several advantages of owning mutual funds. First, they offer you diversification. When you invest in a fund, your money is riding on a large number of securities instead of just a few, which minimizes the risk.

Professional management fees typically run about 1 percent of your investment annually and you can sell your mutual funds any time, just like stocks. If you've invested in one of the funds such as Fidelity Investments' family of funds, you can switch between the different funds in the family as market conditions dictate or your investment objectives change, which give you flexibility.

Finding Good Mutual Funds

There are more than 800 mutual funds to choose from, so choosing the right fund can be a tedious task. How can you quickly go about finding the better funds? Read up. A number of publications out there specialize in investing in funds. *Barron's* magazine and the *Wall Street Journal* publish fund performance data. Use the Internet. *www.morningstar.com,* *www.kiplinger.com,* and *www.investools.com* are three sites to start with. Check the ads. Don't ignore the ads in newspapers and financial magazines. Fund companies like to advertise their better-performing funds.

When you review the prospectus and portfolio of available funds of any mutual fund company, the fund's objective and risk factor will be identified in the prospectus. If you are ready to contact a broker to help you find a suitable fund, here are four brokerage companies that are major players in the mutual fund market:

- Charles Schwab's OneSource fund group (800-435-4000)

- Fidelity's Funds Network (800-544-9697)

- Vanguard Mutual Funds (800-662-7447)

- T. Rowe Price Mutual Funds (800-638-5660)

The mutual fund's fees and expenses are an important part of the decision-making process when choosing which fund to invest in. These charges can lower your return, so you want to be aware of how they work and the impact up front. To help with this, the Security and Exchange Commission has added a cost calculator on its website at *www.sec.gov/investor/tools/rrifcc/mfcc-intsec.htm*. If you link to *www.sec.gov/investor/tools/mfcc/mfcc-int.htm* you will be able to get the answer to this question.

The difference is that when you purchase a no-load fund, you are not charged a sales fee or points when you acquire the fund. Load funds charge sales points. On the surface, no-load funds would appear to be the best choice since no one likes to pay unnecessary sales commissions or fees. However, consider whether it is worth paying a sales fee to acquire a top-grade fund that's producing the returns you want. If you are interested in getting fund research material, consider getting one of the better resources such as Morningstar No-Load Funds newsletter (800-735-0700). It features nearly 700 no-load and low-load mutual funds monthly. Value Line (800-577-4566) is another valuable newsletter that you can try.

Typically, you can buy or sell funds directly through your fund company. However, if the funds were purchased through another source, such as a third-party broker, you can go directly to them, but you will most likely incur a sales charge. To avoid any charges, several financial organizations such as Schwab's One Source,

Vanguard's Fund Access, and Fidelity's Funds Network offer no-charge options.

Investing in Exchange Traded Funds

An exchange traded fund or ETF, like a mutual fund, is an index fund that trades in the market like a stock. ETFs are an attractive alternative to mutual funds because they trade anytime during the trading day when the market is open. In a nutshell, if you put in an order to buy or sell an ETF, the transaction will go through in minutes. They also allow investors to buy shares in a portfolio of a wide variety of stocks and bonds.

Most ETFs are offered on the American Stock Exchange and cover a wide range of diverse investments. For example, if you're interested in diversifying your investment in the NASDAQ exchange, QQQQ is the trade symbol of an ETF that allows you to do that. It's made up of 100 prominent NASDAQ traded stocks. DIA (trade symbol) is the equivalent of QQQQ that covers the primary stocks on the New York stock exchange. There are over 200 ETFs for you to consider. If you are interested in reading more about ETFs, go to *www.investopedia.com*.

ETFs have become extremely popular because owning an ETF allows you the diversification features of a mutual fund while providing the flexibility of trading like a stock. Another reason for their popularity is that ETFs offer investors a way to diversify their investments without having to pay the high premiums that many mutual funds charge. Today, there are more than 200 ETFs that you can buy that cover dozens of market sectors including leisure, semiconductors, health care, oil, precious metals, and networking. There are several types of ETFs that are summarized as follows:

Sector ETFs: Sector ETFs do what their name implies; they restrict investments to a particular industry or sector of the market.

Index ETFs: For many investors, index ETFs are by far the easiest, most effective way to go. If your goal is long-term growth without having to pay much attention, these workhorse funds are the best solution. They simply buy all the stocks in a chosen index (i.e., QQQQDIA, etc.) with the goal of matching that group's performance.

Blend ETFs: These ETFs can go across the board. They might invest in both high-growth tech stocks and communication companies. Because of their mixed blends, they can be difficult to classify in terms of risk.

Value ETFs: Value ETFs like to invest in companies that the market has overlooked. They search for stocks that have become "undervalued" or priced low relative to their earnings potential.

Growth ETFs: As their name implies, growth ETFs tend to look for the fastest-growing companies on the market. Growth ETFs are willing to take more risk in an effort to build a portfolio of companies with above-average momentum or price appreciation.

Micro-cap ETFs: These funds look for companies with market values below $250 million and tend to look for start-up companies that are about to exploit new markets. With stocks this small, the risk is always extremely high, but the growth potential is exceptional.

Small-cap ETFs: A small-cap ETF focuses on companies with a market value below $1 billion. Their volatility often depends on the aggressiveness of their manager. They typically invest in hot growth companies and take high risks in hopes of high rewards.

Mid-cap ETFs: These ETFs fall in the middle of the capital value range. They invest in companies with market values in the $1 to $6 billion range. The stocks at the lower end of their range are likely to exhibit the growth characteristics of smaller companies and therefore add some volatility to these funds.

Large-cap ETFs: These funds focus on companies with a market value above $6 billion. Their volatility is reduced because of the size of the companies that are in their portfolios.

When you invest in a stock-based ETF, you become a shareholder in a portfolio of a variety of stocks. You don't have to worry about the volatility of a single stock since your investment is spread across several stocks. ETFs are among the least time consuming of all investing strategies to maintain. A professional portfolio manager handles all buying and selling of stocks in the fund as well as all the other day-to-day responsibilities, leaving you to do other things, such as playing golf.

Annual expenses for ETFs range between one tenth of a percent to .65 percent versus up to 2 percent for a regular mutual fund. Many investors do not wish to pore over annual reports and would prefer a more passive approach. Because of their relative diversity, ETFs are ideal for investors who lack the time or inclination to select individual stocks. An ETF may be traded any time the exchanges are open. Open-ended mutual funds can only be redeemed at the closing price of the day.

ETFs offer the advantage of diversifying your investment portfolio based on the way these funds work. When you invest in either one, you're buying shares in a portfolio of securities managed by a professional investment firm. Investing in mutual funds and ETFs has proven extremely popular with investors who have minimal time to do their own analysis, are interested in diversification, and need the help of professional experts to choose the right companies to invest in.

ETFs can minimize the risk that follows an investment in an individual stock. For example, buying into the ETF known as the NASDAQI00 Index Tracking Stock (QQQQ2 enables you to share in over 100 companies and diversifies your investment in several industries, so that losses in one are offset by gains in others. By contrast, if you put your entire investment into an individual stock, that stock could go south and take your investment with it.

How Securities Are Traded

The Security and Exchange Commission has a great website that outlines how the trade execution works for stocks, bonds, and funds and what you need to know. By going to *www.sec.gov/investor/pubs/tradexec.htm* you can read about the trading process and gain a better understanding of how it works. The cost or price of a security varies daily depending on market conditions. To determine the current price per share, you look up the daily price of the security of your choice.

Typically, you buy securities through a financial institution that offers brokerage services. However, be aware that full-service brokerage commissions can take a large bite out of your profits. For example, assume that you invest $10,000 in a stock and pay a $200 commission to a full-service broker for the buy order. The price of your stock must increase to $10,200 or 2 percent before you can break even, and then there will be another $200 commission fee when you sell. So technically, your stock price needs to reach $10,400 or increase in value by 4 percent to break even when you sell it in order to recoup both buy and sell commissions.

Get recommendations from friends and associates. What brokers are they using? What do they like and dislike about their brokers? Select a reputable firm that has a good track record. Several financial institutions offer online services that help reduce the commission rates (e.g., charge less than $10 a trade) to investors. It may behoove you to become more familiar with the process by using a full-service broker for your initial trades and then look into their online options such as the one offered at Fidelity Investments.

Tax Implications of Owning Securities

The trick to knowing when to buy or sell stocks, bonds, and funds is to know the tax implications prior to the buy or sale. For example, when you sell a stock at a profit, you incur capital gains taxes, which are calculated based on the amount of time that stock was actually held. As a rule, you want to minimize taxes by recognizing the smallest gain or the largest loss possible on your income tax return. It's always important to understand the tax laws and how to make them work in your favor. Therefore, make sure to consult a tax professional when purchasing or selling stocks that may have significant tax consequences.

Funds can be taxed in three main ways: (1) when you sell the funds for more than you paid for them (2) when the fund yields dividend payments and/or capital gains and (3) when you receive a distribution due to the profitable sale of the fund's securities. Make sure you are aware of how the fund you are considering selling is taxed (i.e., short-term or long-term capital gains) and how it will impact your current taxes.

Many investors have turned to tax-friendly funds to keep Uncle Sam at arm's length. Municipal bond funds are tax-friendly because their interest is exempt from federal taxes and sometimes state and local taxes as well. Vanguard Group has put some emphasis around this over the recent years. You can see their savvy charts that outline the tax benefits of some funds by going to *www.vanguard.com.*

Investing in Annuities

Annuities are hybrid products that combine the advantages of long-term investments with the advantages of life insurance. They are sold like securities by insurance companies. They differ from insurance policies, where you typically pay monthly premiums. With an annuity, you pay a lump sum up front to guarantee a periodic payout immediately or starting at some future date that you choose. Annuity payments continue for as long as you live. Fortunately, people are living longer, which can pose a quandary for those who are worried about outliving their savings. One way to save for retirement and ensure that your money lasts as long as you do is to invest in an annuity. Annuities come in two basic categories: deferred and immediate-income annuities.

A deferred annuity allows you to save money for retirement on a tax-deferred basis until you start withdrawing money from the account. You can choose between a fixed or variable tax-deferred annuity. The variable option allows you to withdraw money from your annuity at whatever amount fits your needs. A fixed annuity allows you to convert your annuity into a "fixed" monthly source of income over your lifetime. The monthly amount is dependent upon your age when you initiate the conversion.

An immediate-income annuity is a contract issued to you by an insurance company that turns a single lump-sum payment into payments (i.e., monthly) over your lifetime or, if you prefer, for a specific number of years. Most annuities offer payment features that cover your spouse after you die. You can opt to receive full or reduced joint income, depending on your situation. Most major life insurance companies offer a variety of annuity products. websites such as *www.annuityshopper.com* offer annuity quotes based on your age and other criteria.

They offer a guaranteed payment amount that's locked in. Although the timing of the payments might vary, depending upon the type of annuity you've selected, the guarantee makes retirement planning easier. They offer insurance in case you outlive your savings. Most annuities offer you a guaranteed payment for life. They offer you tax-deferred income. Annuity income is taxed only when you elect to receive it. Your tax rate is usually lower after you retire.

You'll pay relatively high sales fees when you purchase an annuity. Don't forget that a portion of the purchase price of your annuity goes toward a life insurance policy on you. Only a portion of the purchase price goes toward investments. If you die early, you won't get the full potential of your annuity payout. Most annuities offer a fixed monthly payout that is not adjusted for inflation.

Chapter 5

Banking On Social Security & Medicare

Like coyotes and cockroaches, if there is a nuclear war, both Social Security and Medicare will survive

Despite the spreading fear that social security will fold, be aware that social security is here for the long term. True, the program needs financial bolstering to ensure that there will be sufficient money to cover the surge of baby boomers who are about to tap into the system, but the political consequences of a social security disaster will ensure its survival. So, disregard the rhetoric and start analyzing the benefit you'll get from social security and Medicare to supplement your retirement income.

Enrolling in Social Security

If you have worked for ten or more years and were born on or after 1929, then you are eligible for retirement benefits through social security. The official website for social security has a great tool called the Benefit Eligibility Screening Tool (BEST) that can help you identify which of the different social security programs you may be eligible for. The BEST can be found by going to *www.ssa.gov.* This is a great starting point for understanding your retirement benefits and qualifications.

The government does not automatically enroll anyone in social security, so you have to contact them and complete the necessary applications. You apply for social security three months before you want your benefits to start. When you apply, you will need to submit a completed form, as well as a certified copy of your birth certificate. You can apply online at *www.ssa.gov,* by mail (forms are online), or over the phone at 800-772-1213. You can also report all changes by calling the main number. Typical changes include a new address, new marital status, or returning to work if you were under disability benefits.

What You'll Get

As a general rule, social security will cover about 25 percent of your pre-retirement income (less if you're rich; more if you're poor). Social security uses a formula to calculate what is called your Average Indexed Monthly Earnings (AIME) at retirement. Currently, your payment is based on 90 percent of the first $592 of your monthly income, 32 percent of the next $2,975, and then 15 percent of the amount over $3,567.The maximum monthly benefit you can receive at age 65 is $1,874 per month.

Your social security income is tax-free unless you are married and your annual earnings are more than $32,000 or single with earnings exceeding $25,000, which includes half of your social security income in that total. The percentage of your social security that's taxable grows as your adjusted gross income grows. A maximum of 85 percent will be taxable if your adjusted annual income on a joint return reaches $44,000 ($35,000 for singles). Carefully plan your absences from the work force. If you decide to take time off, be aware that the time you are not working counts against you when your social security benefit is calculated.

If you decide to leave your full-time job, consider working part time to earn money that will count toward your retirement benefit. If you earn less than your spouse, consider taking your benefit at age 62. The spousal benefit is almost always larger if the lower earning spouse had consistently low earnings over a short work life, while the other spouse is on track for maximum benefits. If you are divorced, protect your right to benefits based on your ex-spouse's earnings. You're entitled to social security checks calculated according to your ex-spouse's work history if one-half of their benefit is larger than what you would have received based on your own work history. Call the Social Security Administration (800-772-1213) and ask them to send you form SSA-7004 for your personal earnings and benefits estimate. Start checking their records against your annual W-2 forms to make sure that your benefit earning potential is accurately recorded.

Many individuals decide to retire after 65 years of age. For this reason, social security provides credit to individuals delaying their retirements by increasing the monthly percentage of social security that they will collect once they retire. For example, if you were born between 1933 and 1934, your yearly rate of increase is 5.5 percent and your monthly rate of increase is 11/24 of 1 percent. To find out what rate increase you would receive, go to *www.ssa.gov* . The benefit increase will not apply after you reach the age of 70, even if you decide to delay your benefits. Therefore you should make sure to apply for social security prior to your seventieth birthday.

How Age and Earnings Affect Social Security

Your age and earning level are what determines the amount of social security you are able to collect. You can get a quick estimate of your potential benefit amounts through an online calculator found at *www.ssa.gov/planners/ca/culators.htm*. The calculator is strictly a reference tool to help you determine when you want to retire and help you plan your retirement based on the estimated benefits you may receive.

Your "full retirement age" depends on what year you were born. Depending on your birth year, your full retirement age is anywhere between 65 and 67. To calculate your specific retirement age, go to *www.ssa.gov/pubs/ageincrease.htm*. As mentioned in the previous question, if you decide to retire past your full retirement age, you still qualify for retirement benefits. If you are interested in taking advantage of your social security benefits before that age, you can do so as early as 62 years of age. However, if you opt to begin your plan early, be aware that you will receive a decrease in your monthly social security checks because the program takes into account your age. To better understand the age 62 reduction amounts, review the chart at *www.ssa.gov/retire2/agereduction.htm*.

Earning Extra Income

Once you reach full retirement age, there is no limit on the amount you can earn while collecting social security benefits. However, if you decide to work prior to reaching full retirement age and still collect social security, then you should be aware of what can impact your benefits. If you are under full retirement age, $1 will be deducted from your benefit payments for every $2 you earn above the annual limit. When you reach full retirement age, $1 will be deducted for every $3 earned above a different limit, but it is only counted toward earnings from the month before you reach full retirement age.

Starting with the month you reach full retirement age, you can get benefits with no limit on your earnings. For example, if you were born in 1940, your full retirement age is 65 years and 6 months so you can begin to collect with no limit at 65 years old. If you are interested in getting additional information, visit *www.ssa.gov/retire2/whileworking.htm.*

Once you're on social security, how much are you allowed to earn without incurring a reduction in your social security payment? The answer to this question depends on the individual. You can get your personalized answer by going to the Social Security Administration's website at *www.ssa.gov/retire2/whileworking.htm.* The site provides you with a calculator that will help you in determining your maximum earning potential without incurring a reduction in your monthly social security payment. If you're under "full retirement age," the most you can earn in 2007 without incurring a reduction is $12,960.

Medicare Basics

Medicare goes into effect at the age of 65. If you are collecting social security at full retirement age, then your Medicare hospital benefits start automatically. However, if you are 65 and have not begun to collect social security, you should still sign up for Medicare at the age of 65 to avoid any increases in pricing. There is a list of things that you will need to supply to the Social Security offices when signing up for Medicare. You can go to *www.ssa.gov* to learn more.

Medicare coverage comes in two parts. Part A covers hospital bills and bills from skilled nursing homes, hospice care, and a certain amount of home health care. You pay for this coverage through your social security taxes and are automatically covered beginning at age 65.

Part B is optional and covers doctor bills, outpatient surgery, emergency room treatment, X-rays, laboratory tests, a portion of prescription drugs, and medical equipment such as wheelchairs. When you register for Part A, you will be asked if you want to participate in Part B. The answer should be "yes" unless you have an excellent private insurance policy that covers Part B expenses. A monthly premium for Part B gets deducted from your social security check. However, there are three primary fees that are not covered by Medicare:

- You will pay an up-front deductible fee every time you are hospitalized.

- If you are hospitalized for over ninety days, you will have to pay a daily deductible fee for every day past the ninety day mark.

- Medicare pays 80 percent of physician fees and other medical services. However, you will be responsible for paying the other 20 percent.

If you are on Medicare, select doctors who accept Medicare assignments. That is, they accept whatever Medicare pays and you are, therefore, not responsible for additional fees. You can find supporting doctors by going to *www.medicare.gov* and selecting search tools from their home page. Always check your insurance plan before undergoing elective surgery. Call the insurer to make sure they cover all costs associated with the procedure before you commit to the surgery. Keep records of all phone calls and correspondence with your insurance company concerning the matter. It is highly advisable to get something in writing from your insurance company before you elect any procedures.

If you are paying a portion of the doctor or hospital bill, get an itemized statement that shows exactly what you're paying for. Hospitals are notorious for overcharging patients. If there is a twenty-four-hour emergency clinic in your neighborhood, check out their prices. They're generally cheaper than hospital emergency rooms. If you're overweight and smoke, lose weight and stop smoking. You are much more likely to get reasonable insurance premiums if you are in good health. With a few smart moves, you can cut your prescription drug bills by 50 percent or more. Here's how:

Go generic whenever you can. If your doctor prescribes a brand-name drug, always ask if there is a generic equivalent. Generic drugs are usually known by their chemical names and are virtually identical to the better-known brand-name versions, but offer up to 70 percent in savings.

Look for substitutes. If you're taking a brand-name drug for which no generic is available, ask your doctor or pharmacist if you can switch to a less expensive drug in the same category. In some cases, a substitute may even be available over the counter.

Comparison shop. Prices for the same drug can vary dramatically between pharmacies. Start by checking prices at online pharmacies such as Costco.com, Familymeds.com or Drugstore.com. If you take a certain drug regularly, buying a ninety-day instead of a thirty-day supply can reduce your cost.

Find a good discount drug program. For instance, Partnership for Prescription Assistance *(www.pparx.com; 888-477*-2669) provides a centralized data bank that makes it easy to learn about more than 250 public and private discount drug programs.

Long-term Care Facilities

According to the National Association of Insurance Commissioners, one in every three persons 65 or older will spend some time in a long-term care facility. Not counting the patients who stay three months or less, one out of four will stay for four months to a year. About one out of ten will stay five years or more. The risk is much higher for women than it is for men. Medicare covers the first three months of your stay in a nursing home. After that, you must pay the expenses associated with your care. Statistics show that needing long-term care at some point in your later years is probably inevitable. Thus, you should make it an important consideration for your retirement plan.

You may not need long-term care insurance if you have assets in excess of a million dollars or can afford to pay for a nursing home yourself. If you would rather see your estate passes on to your spouse or kids when you die instead of using your own money to cover the cost of living in a nursing home, consider buying a long-term care policy.

When should you buy long-term care insurance? The younger you are, the cheaper it is. If you buy a policy at 50 and hold it for thirty-five years (to age 85), you will probably pay less for it than if you had bought the same policy at 75 and held it for ten years. Furthermore, you can't buy a policy unless you are in reasonably good health. So the longer you wait, the greater the risk that you won't be insurable.

The two primary types of care facilities are nursing homes and assisted care homes. Both are unique, so it is important to understand their differences. A nursing home is a place where people live on a permanent basis because, for a variety of reasons, they are unable to take care of all their physical needs.

Assisted care homes, sometimes referred to as managed care homes, are a significant step away from nursing homes. People who live in managed care homes are capable of tending to all or most of their physical needs. In a typical care home, residents live in their own apartments and have the option of eating in a central dining facility. Well-run care homes offer a variety of activities for their residents to participate in, such as games, field trips, social gatherings, exercise classes, arts and crafts, and more.

Some things to be aware of with managed care homes are that they limit your medical choices in some ways. For example, although their facility has nursing staff that make themselves available twenty-four hours every day, you are expected to have your own network of doctors that will oversee your care. Should an emergency arise, managed care facilities have an emergency staff and equipped vehicles to transport you to an emergency or medical facility. Also, managed care facilities can cost less than half of what it costs to stay in a nursing home.

Chapter 6

Relocating Options to Consider

There may be a pot of gold at the end of the rainbow if you're willing to relocate

Although you probably bought your home years ago, thanks to inflation you've ended up with an asset that's worth a lot more than what you paid for it. The opportunity to leverage the equity you've built up in your home is an important part of the foundation of your retirement plan. As you approach retirement, consider these options when you evaluate whether you should keep or sell your home:

Consider trading down. Estimate your profit before you consider selling. What will it cost for an acceptable replacement? If the potential profit from selling your home is minimal, it might not be worth the effort of trading down.

Time the sale of your home to take advantage of tax breaks .If you or your spouse is age 55 or older, you can exclude from taxes up to $500,000 of the capital gains on the sale of your home.

Consider keeping your home and refinancing it with an individual reverse mortgage (IRM) or a leaseback. In this arrangement, a lender receives part or all of the equity in your home, in return for payments that you receive for the rest of your life.

Sell your home and move to apart of the country where the costs of housing and living are lower. Not only will you get more home for your money, you may also get the added benefit of a lower cost of living in the new area.

Getting the Most Out of Your Home

The house you have always dreamed of may be the one you already live in. Maybe you're thinking of a spacious living room, a modern kitchen, or an extra bath. If so, turning your vision into reality may simply be a matter of remodeling your present house. But, whatever you do, you want to make sure you can get your money back out of your investment should you decide to sell your home.

Consider high-rate returns on things you decide to remodel. Popular improvements such as remodeling a bath or a kitchen add the most value and will usually yield great returns when you sell your home. Installing energy-improvement devices are always a good way to reduce your monthly energy costs. Don't install expensive energy-efficient devices unless you plan to stay in your home for at least another three years.

Don't over-improve. Consider the value of your home in your neighborhood if you'd have to price your home significantly above the average price range in your neighborhood. Consider what your house looks like on the outside. Make sure it has curb appeal or the potential for curb appeal with minor enhancements. Home maintenance projects, such as roof repair and replacement, are essential whether or not you're anticipating selling your home. *The Home Remodeling Organizer* by Robert Irwin discusses various remodeling projects from a practical perspective. Also check out *Squeeze Your Home for Cash: 101 Great Money-Making Ideas for Homeowners* by Ruth Rejnis.

Paying Off Your Mortgage

Nothing can save you more money than paying off your home mortgage as soon as you can. Typically, people opt for thirty-year mortgages because that gives them plenty of time to pay off their homes, while offering them lower monthly payments. However, if you can work it into your budget to have a higher monthly mortgage in order to pay off your home faster, then do so.

If you're buying a house or own a home with a thirty-year mortgage with no prepayment penalties (most don't have them), consider what a fifteen-year mortgage can do for you. For example, if you have a $200,000 thirty-year 7 percent mortgage, your payments are approximately $1,400 a month. If you finance the same amount for fifteen years, your payments would be $1,700 a month. For a difference of only $300 a month, you can pay for your house outright in half the time. If you have a good interest rate with your current thirty-year loan, then consider paying an extra payment each year and you will expedite paying off your home, which can catapult your early retirement ambitions.

One of the best ways to pay down your current loan is to make extra payments on your existing loan. If you decide to do this, make sure your lender understands that the extra money you're paying should be applied against the principle and not applied toward a noninterest-bearing impound account, which lenders would prefer. If you can't afford to make the extra monthly payments, make just one extra payment per year, and you'll drop years off your thirty-year mortgage. If you want to read more about the advantages of paying off your home earlier than expected, as well as understanding all the types of loans available, then consider reading *The Banker's Secret* by Marc Eisenson.

Refinancing Your Home

Mortgage loan experts will tell you to consider refinancing your mortgage when interest rates drop 2 percentage points below your current rate. Before you pursue a refinance option, you need to get answers to several questions from prospective lenders:

1. Given the current rates, how much will you save each month after you refinance?

2. How much will it cost to refinance and will you be in your home long enough to make it worthwhile?

3. Is the term of the proposed refinance plan the same as or less than your current mortgage term?

If you want to compare the effect of different interest rates and terms, run your current mortgage figures through a mortgage calculator found at *www.mortgage-calc.com.Then* run the new figures you're considering to see if they make sense. You need to understand several terms when going through the loan or refinance process. We have listed a few terms to help get you started:

Terms. A term is the amount of time that is set for the repayment of the mortgage or loan. Typically a term ranges from fifteen to thirty years. Review the rate and term of any new loan you're considering. One lender may offer you a lower interest rate but a longer term. Another may offer you a higher rate but shorter term. Shop around and make sure you are comparing apples with apples to find the best deal.

Closing costs. Some mortgage companies offer loans with no closing costs, which are costs owed during the closing of the property. Generally speaking, you'll pay higher interest, but if you're not sure how long you'll be in your home, this may be a good deal. Check the fine print to make sure there are no early prepayment penalties in case you decide to sell.

Loan options. Some mortgage companies offer streamlined loans that allow you to get better rates and terms without having to go through all the expensive steps of closing associated with a new appraisal. You'll end up paying lower closing costs but potentially a higher interest rate.

Modified loans. Your existing mortgage company may offer you a modified loan. They may be willing to change your loan rate and/or term by simply modifying your existing loan. Subsequently, a new loan does not need to be created and there is no closing, which eliminates closing costs.

One thing you can look into is writing off points on your tax return when you refinance. Usually the points paid to a mortgage company must be written off over the life of the new loan. But if you refinance a second time before all of the points are written off on your original loan, you can deduct the entire remaining balance in the year that you refinanced. The write-off could amount to several thousands of dollars.

To learn more, reference Julie Garton-Good's book *All About Mortgages: Insider Tips to Finance a Home,* which covers everything you need to know about home mortgages. Another excellent reference is *Your Home Mortgage Answer Book: 100 Questions and the Answers You Need* by Mary Callegari, which covers refinancing and mortgage insurance questions. And finally, *The Mortgage Kit* by Thomas Steinmetz and Phillip Whitt gives you a comprehensive guide to everything you ever wanted to know about mortgages.

Relocation Options

There are some wonderful places to retire in America, and the list gets broader and broader every year. The best way to begin your quest is to identify some areas of interest. A variety of hot spots have popped up all over the United States that are geared toward the retirement population.

Money magazine publishes an annual edition that covers the best places to retire in America. The magazine polled its readers to determine where the baby boomers want to retire. The number-one choice for the readers was to stay in their current location. The runner-up was to move closer to their children. The third choice was to have a second home. Whatever scenario fits your bill, knowing your options is key in your decision-making process.

To help you determine what areas interest you, take a few minutes to complete the quiz found at *www.findyourspot.com.* The quiz takes you through a series of questions to help narrow your results to areas that might appeal to you. Don't forget, you now have the time to check out each area if you want. You can even spend some time at each destination and really determine whether the community is right for you.

A helpful resource that will give you options to consider geographically is at *Money's* website (www.money.com) that offers several tools to get you started on your quest. You can enter cities and find out all the statistical information you need. For example, a search on San Diego, California provides the population of the city, median price for a house, the best and worst areas to live in, etc. You can also check out the retirement sections of the site and determine how much you could sell your house for, learn how to find your dream home, and much more.

If you are a United States citizen, then you can freely travel or live in most foreign countries without affecting your social security benefits. If you are living in a foreign country, you may be able to get payments directly to your foreign address. However, the list of qualifying countries changes daily, so it's important to read more about your place of residency and how your social security benefits work. Call social security at 800-772-1213 for more information.

Finding a Good Deal

Consider buying a "fixer-upper" if you are handy with tools and paintbrushes. A structurally sound house that is priced 20 to 30 percent below market because it needs some "tender loving care" could be a good investment. Look for distress situations where a seller has to put a house on the market for a quick sale because of a job transfer, divorce settlement, or foreclosure to settle an estate. Here are some tips for finding a good deal on a home:

Anybody who's thinking about a home mortgage should be prepared to shop aggressively. Some lenders have drastically lower rates and fees than others, especially for preferred borrowers. One percentage point saved on a fifteen-year, $200,000 loan is worth $36,720, or about $210 a month.

Mortgage banks are usually the cheapest route to go. Their main business is mortgages, including those that are backed by the Federal Housing Administration or the Department of Veterans Affairs. Credit unions are your next-best bet, although only the larger ones offer mortgages. Next, try savings and loan banks and associations followed by commercial banks. As in any field, some mortgage brokers are more competent and attentive than others. And don't be afraid to shop the Web. Many national and regional mortgage banks advertise their rates and services complete with applications online.

Getting a Home Loan

The first thing is to understand the loans that will be offered to you. Most homes are financed with loans secured by a deed of trust, commonly referred to as a mortgage. Mortgages are available from many sources, including commercial banks, savings and loan associations, credit unions, insurance companies, and mortgage companies. Most lenders offer fully amortized loans in which you repay the principle (borrowed amount) and the interest over a specified period of time. At first, most of your payment goes toward the interest.

As you continue to make payments over time, an increasing part of your payment goes to pay off the principle and a decreasing part goes to the interest. Interest is either fixed or variable. Fixed rate loans are where the interest rate and your monthly payments remain the same over the term of the loan, which is usually thirty years. Variable-rate loans offer an interest rate that fluctuates with the market interest rate. They are usually indexed to the prime rate plus points. The prime rate is the preferred interest rate that is offered by lending institutions to their best corporate customers. The prime rate will fluctuate up or down at any point in time with changes in the economy.

A point is equivalent to one interest point, so if a bank offers you a variable-rate mortgage at prime plus two points, and prime is at 6 percent, you'll pay 8 percent interest. If the prime increases to 7 percent next month, you'll pay 9 percent interest. Because of the variable fluctuations, you need to proceed with caution when choosing this type of loan.

If you want to see what resources are available online, E- Loan at *www.eloan.com* offers mortgages from sixty lenders to home buyers in thirty-nine states. Home Shark at *www.homeshark.com* provides a service that is similar to E- Loan. They represent sixteen lenders who operate out of forty-six states. Quicken Loans at *www.quickenloans.com* offers a service that lets you compare rates and terms with eleven national lenders.

Renting Versus Buying

According to the late Andrew Carnegie "ninety percent of all millionaires became so through owning real estate. He went on to state that "more money has been made in real estate than in all industrial investments combined." What Carnegie, as well as other investors, would tell you is to buy a home if you don't already have one. Wells Fargo has an extensive site about home buying, including workshops and seminars for the prospective home buyer. To help you get started, go to *www.wellsfargo.com/challenge.*

On the contrary, if you decide to rent, understand that you are paying someone else's mortgage and helping her to experience the appreciation and tax advantages on the property. However, renting is sometimes advantageous when you move to a new area and are not sure where you want to live, or if you decide to build a house and need temporary shelter during the process. We don't rule out renting because it really depends on your situation and needs. We just suggest that you weigh the pros and cons of owning versus renting to determine what solution works best for you in retirement.

Condominiums Versus Homes

Condominiums are attached to one another, thereby sharing common walls. You own a unit and share common grounds such as recreational areas with the other condominium owners through what is called a homeowners' association. One of the major advantages condominiums have over freestanding homes is that they generally cost less to buy and require less upkeep. Each owner pays a monthly maintenance fee to the homeowners' association to maintain the exterior walls of each condominium, provide landscaping services, and pay for some form of homeowner's insurance.

Condominium covenants typically have a long list of things you can and can't do as an owner. If you don't like regulations, don't buy a condominium. For retired people, condos offer a comfortable step back from what it takes to care for a home. Security is generally tighter in a condominium complex than it is around a private home because of the close proximity of neighbors. Some condominiums have twenty-four-hour security guards on the premises.

Single-family homes generally have a greater potential for capital appreciation than condominiums if they're located in an area where property values have consistently risen over the past several years.

Quite often, small investments in cosmetic improvements such as paint and landscaping can substantially improve their selling price. They offer more privacy than what you will find in a condominium since you are not in such close proximity to your neighbors. And if gardening and landscaping is your forte, then a home with a backyard might be better for you. However, since you are responsible for all upkeep on a home, you can expect to spend more to maintain a home than you would a condominium. The decision ultimately comes down to personal preference. You really can't go wrong with either one. You have to weigh it all out and determine what's right for you.

Retirement Communities

Throughout the country, retirement communities have popped up that offer all levels of care for the aging population. With a boomer turning age 50 every eight seconds, the demand for these retirement developments has skyrocketed. One site that can help you search the market is *www.seniorhousingnet.com.* The site offers a one-stop shop for resources on retirement. It provides information and tips about housing, moving, financing, and specialized care and is a wealth of knowledge at your fingertips.

Chapter 7

Traveling Ways

You can improve the quality of your life by traveling and you will live longer

Enjoy yourself and make fun a priority during your retirement. You've worked hard and now you get to reap the benefits. Take on an adventure and go beyond the ordinary to seek out the joys of retirement. The best aspect of traveling during retirement is that you can choose the optimal time to visit popular destinations and miss the traffic that comes with peak season vacations. Hotels, museums, movie theaters, and other places offer discounts to the older population. For example, if you are 62 or older, the U.S. Forest Service will offer you a lifetime pass to all the national parks for only $15. If you're a bargain hunter and like to save, then you need to step forward and admit that you deserve the senior citizen discount. You can go to *www.seniordiscounts.com* or *http://frugalliving.about.com/od/seniorcitizens* to find out more about some great discounts.

There are several sources of information that can help you choose your next trip or hot spot to visit. If you want to make traveling top on your priority list, then consider getting a monthly subscription to a travel magazine. *Budget Travel* is an excellent travel magazine that features the latest travel bargains. It provides budget-saving solutions to anywhere you may want to go. There's a section that lists the special deals that are going on each month with related websites and contacts to get more information.

Where to Travel

There is a great website that can help you find your next destination at *traveldiscovery*.com. This website has a listing of the best beaches, boardwalks, theme parks, water parks, scuba diving, light house tours, California wine tours, popular destinations, and much more. Hotels are not always the most comfortable or economical means for traveling. In fact, many retirees are looking to stay longer at their featured destination and don't want to pay the expensive prices offered through hotels. There are many other options to help make your stay more enjoyable and easier on your wallet. For instance, house-swapping has become extremely popular. Inter-vacation *(www.intervac.com)* is an organization that was started in 1953 by Swiss and Swedish teachers. They currently have over 11,000 homes in more than fifty countries around the world. The fee to join their organization online is only $79 for a year or $129 to receive their catalog.

Another option would be to join an organization called the Evergreen Club *(evergreenclub.com)*. The club consists of more than 2,000 members who have signed up to play host during short visits by other travelers in the club. For as little as $15 a day per couple, you can stay for up to three nights in another member's guest room, and breakfast is included.

If you're interested in group trips, look no further than AARP's passport tours. The organization is focused on persons 50 and older and helps put trip packages together that meet the needs of seniors who are interested in traveling around the world. They offer substantial discounts through their last-minute packages as well. You can see all that the program has to offer by going to their travel link at *www.aarp.organdgoing*. Another great resource that caters to Americans over 50 is Grand Circle Travel. You can get a free catalog and more information by going to *www.gct.com*.

Traveling on a Budget

Credit cards offer some wonderful opportunities for you to earn free airline miles. Many offer programs in which you get a flier mile for every dollar you spend. Sometimes, the cards will offer promotional deals for first-time users that include airline tickets, free companion passes, bonus miles, etc. Visit individual airlines' websites for further travel details. To help minimize your costs for travel, read Lynie Arden's book *Travel Free: The Ultimate Guide to Bargain*

Travel. It is packed with information on how to travel inexpensively or free.

One great website to look at is Travelocity at *www.travelocity.com.* The site has information on flights, hotels, vacation packages, car rentals, and just about anything you'll need to plan your next vacation or business trip. Also, check out *www.besifares*.com, *www.budgettravelcom,* and *www.cheapertravelcom.* Another quick promotional check would be through your local newspaper. Several major newspapers have a travel section that features travel destinations at special discount prices. Typically, they will have travel inserts in their Sunday papers that feature current deals and promotions. Also checkout travel sites at *www.elderhostel.com, www.tripspot.com/senior,* and *www.aarp.org/travel*

The major airlines make more than 20,000 fare changes each day, so getting the cheapest fare requires careful planning. Look for airfare bargains right after major holidays. Believe it or not, the summer is a great time to find airfare deals. Business travel falls off during the summer and airlines are hustling to fill their planes. You can get the best airfare deals if you buy your tickets at least twenty one days in advance.

Wherever you go, always try to stay over on a Saturday, which can dramatically reduce your fare. If you are flying to attend a funeral, ask the airline about their bereavement policy, which could cut the fare considerably. Travel during the off-season. It's the best time to go anywhere and you can save 40 percent or more on your vacation. Often if you catch the front or tail end of the prime season, you get good rates, no crowds, and good weather. Typically, you will know when offseason starts because you get discounted rates. For example, Florida's peak season is the summer months. However, locals tell us that April and September are less crowded, have great weather, and feature cheaper hotel rates.

Resorts, Cruises and Clubs

Many useful sites and resources are available for you at no cost. If a destination sounds appealing to you and you think a hotel or resort looks charming, then consider checking out personalized reviews at _www.tripadvisor.com_. This site allows people to post their reviews on several hotels and resorts all over the world. They are honest and blunt. It also rates the location against other hotels and resorts in the area, which is helpful when your research gets overwhelming.

To get a fantastic cabin and a good rate, schedule your cruise way in advance through a travel agent who specializes in cruise travel. Cruising is a whole different ball game than other types of travel. Whether you are sailing to Alaska or the Caribbean, if you book your cruise as far as a year ahead, you'll save 30 percent or more. However, you can also get some great last-minute deals on cruises. The nice thing about cruises is that you typically get the food, lodging, and entertainment at one package price.

If you are really into traveling, then consider joining a travel club. Yes, you'll pay an annual fee, but because of their buying power, major travel clubs get access to tremendous travel packages that can exceed 50 percent off retail prices. When you join a club, you get a membership card, a directory showing where you can go at discounted rates, as well as newsletters that announce travel bargains. Major warehouse retailers such as Costco and Sam's Club offer travel discounts to their members.

If you're interested in an adventure travel tour, REI is a great company that offers adventure travels, as well as retail gear for sale through their website, _www.rei.com_. For more than twenty years, they have been offering adventures in hiking, cycling, paddling, camping, and more. It may also behoove you to check with your local travel agencies. Many agencies are popping up around the nation, focusing on recreational and adventure travel.

Using Travel Agents

Planning for your next vacation can be an exciting and yet, an overwhelming experience. By using a travel agent, you are utilizing the expertise and knowledge of a professional. Often the travel agent has been to the destination, or knows about the destination, that you are interested in. He can give you personalized advice that caters to your needs.

A good travel agent will let you know, in advance, when bargain fares are about to be announced. The other benefit to using an agent is that he has access to computer software that ensures you're getting the best airfare available, not just the best deal your agent could find at the time you booked your reservation. Agents can also be of great help in finding destinations that offer handicapped accessibility.

Owning a Vacation Home

Owning a second home has become an alluring prospect for many retirees since the tax changes in 1997 took effect, which allows second-home owners to deduct interest payments and property taxes. In addition, many banks are now more willing to make loans on second homes. As people retire, the thought of purchasing recreational properties, motor homes, and time-shares comes to mind and seems more appealing. In fact, in 2004, second-home sales went up 16 percent from the previous year, according to the National Association of Realtors. This chapter will help answer common questions to assist you in choosing a recreational property, investing in a time-share, or buying a motor home.

Recreational property is generally thought of as real property that people enjoy because of its recreational features. It could be raw land that you use for camping or a swank condominium in Hawaii. In recent years, recreational property has become very popular with retirees who have dreamed about owning a place where they can "get away from it all." If you're thinking about buying a weekend getaway, make sure you buy one that you will really use on a regular basis. The last thing you want to happen is to buy a place that, for whatever reason, you don't use.

 To help avoid this possibility, thoroughly check out any location you're considering and stay there for as many weekends as it takes to make sure it's the right area for you. If you plan to rent the property when you're not using it, check the tourism and hotel occupancy rates with the local chamber of commerce to get a feel

77

for the short-term rental market. Then consider how often you plan to use it. Assuming that you do not plan to use it full-time, will the property be safe from theft and vandalism when you're not there? Can it be insured? Can it be rented when you're not using it to provide you with an added source of income? Is it easy to get to and will the accommodations meet your needs as you age?

It is possible to find a second home that you visit once a year for vacation and rent out to tourists for the rest of the year at rental rates that cover your expenses. High-traffic tourist areas are ideal for this situation. However, bear in mind that IRS rules for this type of property can get complicated. If you use the house for fewer than fifteen days a year or less than 10 percent of the rental period, then it's considered a rental by the IRS. Your deductible expenses can't exceed your rental income.

Before the capital gains tax rules changed in 1997, many people didn't purchase retirement homes until they sold their primary residence so they could roll over any gains from the sale of their current home into the new home. Today there is no need to wait, because the new law allows couples to roll over up to $500,000 of gain ($250,000 for singles) on their primary homes whenever they sell. If you're looking for a place that you can vacation in now and move to later, look at areas that have good health care facilities. If you plan to rent the property, does the area you are considering support a good job market and renter population? Look for states that have relatively low or no state income taxes, which can put money back into your pocket when you move.

Time Shares

When you purchase a time-share property, you technically own a "piece of time" in a particular complex or condominium. Essentially, you buy the right to vacation in the same or similar unit during a specified period of time every year (typically one to two weeks). For this privilege, you pay a purchase price and maintenance fees for your share of the ownership. Most desirable time-shares are located in preferred locations. Then, depending on the unit you purchase, you may also have additional fees to cover maintenance, management, and upkeep costs associated with the complex that your unit is in. The extra fees should be disclosed at the time of purchase, and you should consider these when making a purchasing decision.

If you are only interested in staying at a vacation property you own for a couple of weeks each year, you may want to consider buying into a time-share rather than buying a second home. Time-shares may be appealing, but watch out for the high sales costs. For example, if you buy into a $10,000 time-share and decide to sell your share later, selling and marketing fees can easily be 40 percent or more of the sales price. A word of caution: The timeshare resale market is almost nonexistent, so don't think of a time-share as an investment. Before you buy, consider a consultation with a Realtor to discuss the resale value.

Depending on the specifics of the investment deal you make, you can have limited to very flexible ownership in your share. With flexible time-shares, you can trade your time with other individuals and not be tied down to using your share at a particular time. You can also purchase a fixed unit for a specified period of time each year that's written up in a deed agreement. Another option is a floating time-share arrangement where your time has more flexibility, but you are subject to reservations. This may provide a more feasible solution, but you may end up with scheduling conflicts, since it is based on a first-come, first-served scenario. A third option is a right-to-use agreement that mimics a lease. You have the rights to the unit until your lease expires. After that, you no longer have access to the unit.

The most flexible option is known as vacation clubs. This is a point-based system where you can choose from a variety of locations that are within the club you have purchased the timeshare with. Each of your stays at a club location requires you to use points. These points fluctuate depending on the time of year, the quality of the unit, and/or the location. Major corporations, such as Starwood Hotels and Resorts, use point-based programs to capture interested customers. Typically, you will go through a separate time-share agency that assists with the negotiation of points and planning for your usage.

Advantages and Disadvantages of Timeshares

Once you own it, the cost of staying in your time-share is usually cheaper than renting a comparable unit. You have the opportunity to meet and make friends with other time-sharers who stay in their units at the same time you do. Many time-shares allow you to swap your unit with someone else's at a different location. Owning a time-share can also yield tax breaks because it mimics the taxes associated with owning a second home.

If you don't buy a good time-share in a desirable location, you may have a problem swapping it for another time-share or selling it in the future. If, for whatever reason, your desires change and you stop using your time-share, you will be paying for a vacation that you no longer take. Monthly principle payments and maintenance fees keep on accruing, whether you use it or not. Most people do not make money when they sell their timeshares. Sales fees can run 25 percent or more, so watch out. If you decide to buy into a time-share, it is very important that you do your research. You want to be familiar with the laws associated with time-share property in the state where you are looking to purchase. You may also want to compare pricing and involve a Realtor to assist with this process.

Several resources are available to assist you with your research. For example, the Timeshare Users Group *(www.tug2.net)* offers a variety of topics online such as frequently asked questions, tips, advice, and much more. There are also several books available that can help you understand the basics of buying a time-share. Try *The New Vacation Revolution* by Alexander Barbara (and see his site at *www.vacationrevolution.com)* or *Timeshare Condominiums for the Beginner* by Michael Strauss to grasp the concepts and get your questions answered.

The better you understand time-sharing, the better negotiator you will be and the better deal you will be able to walk away with. There are several different alternatives you can opt for and it is necessary to thoroughly understand all of the options to make the best choice for your circumstances.

Buying a RV

If you are thinking about buying an RV, there are several issues to consider for this big purchase so that you can avoid any pitfalls. You'll need to understand the finance options for RVs, decide whether to buy a new or used, and whether to buy a RV motor home or trailer. The Better Business Bureau has put out a DVD to help first-time buyers through the process. The DVD, *Buying a Recreation Vehicle,* offers straightforward and professional guidance to help consumers make the right decisions and usually save money without running into heartaches along the way. This DVD is available for $19.95 through *www.rvbookstore.com.*

You need to consider the insurance, payments, and possible financing for the model you prefer. The insurance for an RV will vary based on the anticipated usage, your past driving record, and other factors. To get an idea of the costs, you can go to *www.progressive.com,* *www.rv-insurancecoverage.com* or *www.rvinsurance.com.* Also, check with your current insurance provider to see if you can get a multiple-vehicle discount. To determine your financing options, ask whether there are any incentives through the RV dealer. You can also go to *www.rvusa.com* to see a list of financial groups.

Another expense to consider is maintenance. You can plan for the maintenance expense by budgeting the expected yearly fees associated with the anticipated maintenance. You may also opt to purchase an extended warranty on your RV. You may decide to go with a basic RV that meets your needs and will not break your budget for repairs. For example, a newer pop-up trailer is going to require less maintenance than an RV that has 100,000 miles on it. Finally, you will have general usage expenses. These include, but are not limited to, fuel, campground fees, food and supplies, and activity fees. To find out more about the overall expenses associated with RV living, go to *www.your-rv-lifestyle.com.*

As gas prices go up, so does the cost of operating your RV. The best way to prepare for RV ownership is to budget for your personalized costs of usage. One thing that you may want to do when determining your usage budget is list the trips you plan to make and figure the gas cost based on the mileage of the trips. If you will need to store your RV, you will need to include the monthly fee for storage in your budget. Another factor to be calculated is the trip-planning details. If you are planning to stay in campgrounds, you will need to include the fees. If you plan to do certain activities at different destinations, you may want to calculate those costs into your budget. And don't forget, if you finance the RV, you will be making monthly payments. These are just a few of the costs to think about and include in your budget to make sure it aligns with your retirement plan.

Chapter 8

Continuing Your Education

Abraham Lincoln once said "whatever you decide to do, be good at it"

Your pending retirement may open up the time you've always wanted to continue your education. The educational path can take a variety of twists and turns, depending on your specific interests and desires. For example, you may decide to take a class in digital photography so that you can explore all of the features of that new digital camera that you just got. Or you may decide to pursue that college degree that you have always wanted. A recent study by AARP discovered that 73 percent of the baby boomers polled expect to have a hobby or special interest take up most of their retirement. That means that of the baby boomers reaching retirement, 55 million are seeking training for some sort of special interest.

Retirement is a great time to review your hobby interests. If you're struggling with hobby ideas, two websites can help you. The first, *www.hobbylobby.com* is a great website that offers all sorts of hobby interests and products. If gardening is of interest, then click on *www.hgtv.com.* You may also want to check out the different classes available through your local recreational center and any organizations that offer classes of interest. Another suggestion is to check out your local community college website to see what classes they may be offering.

Getting Started

Many schools offer additional services to meet the needs of their aging student populations including financial aid, support groups, and academic assistance, to name a few. In fact, many schools offer online and evening courses to cater to working adults and students with special needs. You will have to check with your institution of choice to determine its specific services.

There are many criteria you want to consider when determining the right school for you. For example, some things that might be on your list are the size of the classrooms, the structure and curriculum, and the school's accreditation. A very useful website that can help narrow your search for colleges is at *www.collegeboard.com*. They have a college matchmaker tool that will help you identify a school that is right for you based on your criteria. If you already have a school in mind, then you can use their college quick finder to get additional information on the college's profile. Both search options are found on the site's home page.

Several mainstream universities offer virtual education through the Internet. Classes are videotaped and can, along with reading and assignments, be accessed online. Often you can take a class in the comfort of your own home at any hour of the day or night! Call or search the website of local universities or colleges to see if they offer online education courses. In addition, universities have popped up everywhere that caters to the working adult who prefers a classroom with more mature adults sharing real-life experiences and pursuing a higher education. If this level of education sounds appealing to you in your retirement, then consider the University of Phoenix, which is one of the more successful adult education programs in the nation. They offer online degree programs, as well as instructor-led programs. You can further research their program and curriculum at *www.uofphx.info*. There are also a variety of different colleges that offer many online programs. A good website to reference is *www.classesusa.com*.

Perhaps you have come to realize that you have always put your dream job on the back burner. Possibly your interest in design, cookery, or art has intrigued you to look into a specialty school. There are a lot of different trade schools that cater to your every wish. You can begin your search by clicking on *www.collegesurfing.com*. This site allows you to search for your career of interest and finds colleges in the area where you live.

Financial Aid Programs

Continuing education has never been cheap, and finding the means to make it work can be a challenge. In their book *501 Ways for Adult Students to Pay for College,* Gen and Kelly Tanabe cover many new college programs set up for the aging population. For example, Oregon has the Senior Adult Learning Center program that does not yield credit hours, but does allow senior citizens to audit any Portland State University class as long as there is available space. If you want to find out specific information about the financial aid you may be eligible for, you can go to *wwwjinaid.org.* This site outlines the different types of aid and some of the factors you will need to consider when filing for aid. It can also answer questions about tax implications and what approach is right for you.

Another option is to call the U.S. Department of Education (800-433-3243) and ask them to send you an application for federal student aid. Study the application and become familiar with the questions you'll be required to answer so that you won't shortchange yourself. For example, a 401(k) plan or pension plan doesn't count as part of your current assets, so don't list them. As a general rule, approximately 6 percent of your assets and up to 50 percent of your income will be considered available for college expenses. Always keep those percentages in mind when you fill out the applications. The entire process can be a bit overwhelming. To help walk you through it, consider getting a copy of *Complete Idiot's Guide to Financial Aid for College* by David Rye.

It's important to have the tools necessary to get the most out of being an older student. Many colleges offer senior programs with great incentives. You can check with the admissions office at your local college to determine which programs are offered. Online studies are becoming very popular so you don't have to physically go to campus. If this is of interest to you, check the school's accreditation first at *www.chea.org* and then go to the websites of colleges you like to find out more about their online programs.

Many colleges offer a wide range of assistance to help you get your feet on the ground and running. You can talk to the admissions office to get information on remedial classes, and to see if they have any senior support groups. Don't think it's too late to study abroad. Although you won't receive college credit, you can still participate in the program and take an Elderhostel trip. The prices vary based on the trip; you can get more information at *www.elderhostelorg.*

Expanding Your Computer Expertise

As more and more seniors go into retirement, the need to stay abreast and connected becomes extremely relevant in the fast-paced world of computers. Some retirees may be extremely comfortable with computers, while others might need some updating of their skills. Several corporations offer online training for free or at a minimal cost. For example, if you want to learn the latest computer innovations, take IBM's online PC basics course geared to the entry-level computer owner. To access the training and get more information, go to w*ww.pc.ibm.com/training.*

Another company that offers specialized training is Dell. Their affordable PC training can be accessed online and they give you up to a year to complete your scheduled course. To view their selection and pricing, go to *www.dell.com* and type "online training" in the Search box. If you prefer hands-on training, then consider looking into your local community college for PC courses. Whatever training method you choose, you can't go wrong with becoming familiar and comfortable with your personal computer. The technology is constantly changing, and it is always a benefit to stay ahead of the game. If you master your computer, you'll know how to make the most of its features and functions to meet your retirement needs.

Connecting to the Web

The Web is a magnificent tool that is literally at your fingertips. Our book references websites throughout because the Web is an extremely useful tool for gathering information. To feel more confident using the Web, it is best that you understand how the technology works. Several online resources can assist all levels of Web users. These resources can walk you through how the Internet works. One particular site, *www.weblearning.net* offers easy-to-follow instructions for beginners. The site shows you how to connect your computer to the Internet, how to use the Web, and how to set up a website, and it offers useful tips and techniques to better understand and use the Internet.

For the intermediate Web user, learning about the latest technologies might be of interest. Wireless networking has taken the industry by storm. Consumers want to be able to access the Internet from anywhere. Therefore, you are starting to see phones and other handheld devices that offer the portability of the Web. Many coffee shops and restaurants offer wireless Internet to their customers for free.

Want to snag a $1,000 suit for $150? Try *www.ebay.com*. If you want to sell something, post it on *www.craigslist.com*. If you're looking for a hard-to-find anthropology book, connect to *www.amazon.com*. You can even have your groceries delivered right to your door by *www.peapod.com*. Let's say you want to get technical product information and compare the specifications of several brands before you buy something. Try *www.compare.netforafreeonlinebuyers.guide* that allows you to compare thousands of products. Other websites to visit are summarized as follows:

Computer Hardware & Software
www.cnet.com
www.newegg.com
www.insight.com

Buying and Selling Goods
www.ebay.com
www.craigslist.com

Music
www.amazon.com
www.apple.com/itunes
www.columbiahouse.com

Books
www.musicblvd.com
www.amazon.com
www.halfebay.com
www.barnesandnoble.com

Senior Informational Sites
www.aarp.org
www.seniors-site.com
www.semor.com
www.senior-center.com

Cars
www.autobytelcom
www.carsmart.com
www.edmunds.com

Greeting Cards
www.bluemountainarts.com
www.evite.com
www.hallmark.com

Take advantage of e-Mail; it's one of the greatest benefits of online technology. Most Internet service providers (ISPs) give their users free e-Mail accounts with a certain amount of storage space for their mail. If you feel you need more storage space than the allotted free space, you can either purchase additional space or download your e-Mail to your desktop to free up space on your account. Each provider will offer specific information about the terms of their email accounts. If you don't like the style of e-rnail that your ISP offers, you can open a free account through some of the more popular Web portals such as Yahoo and Hotmail *(www.hotmail.com).* Either way, e-rnail is a great tool to send mail quickly and at no additional cost.

Chapter 9

Protecting Your Estate

If you're not willing to protect what you have, nobody else will

If you planned it right, your retirement accounts will outlive you. In this chapter, we show you how to create an estate plan so your heirs will receive as much of your hard-earned cash as possible. There are special estate tax benefits that can be extended to your family. Making a will is not difficult, but it is undeniably a serious and sobering process. Never underestimate what your estate is worth. Many people get caught up with the routine of just trying to make a living and struggling to pay the bills to the point where they grossly underestimate the size of their estates. As a result, they fail to take appropriate tax-saving steps. Taxable estates include home equity, retirement-account balances, life insurance proceeds, securities, and other assets. Make sure you know your true worth and assess it accordingly in your estate plan.

Estate Plan Basics

An estate plan arranges for the distribution of assets in your estate when you die or if you are incapacitated. It can be used to make your wishes known regarding your finances and personal care. Most estate plans begin with a will, which specifies who gets your property when you die.

A will combined with a living trust allows you to spell out what you want under specific circumstances like medical treatment while you're still alive. For example, you can specify whether you want life-support equipment under certain medical conditions so that your family members don't have to make that difficult decision on your behalf. Whatever you own at your death is called your estate and can also include:

- Making arrangements for the care of love ones in the event of your death.
- Planning for your own care in case someday you can't make decisions on your own
- Taking steps so your inheritors can avoid probate court proceedings and avoid estate tax.

Everything that you own when you die including your 401(k) and IRA is part of your estate. If it's not left to your spouse, it could be taxed under the estate tax rules. Beneficiaries have immediate access to the retirement account(s) you leave with them, regardless of their ages. If you manage your retirement accounts correctly, beneficiaries may be able to keep the money in your retirement accounts and enjoy the tax benefits. Your estate plan is the final component in your retirement plan. It's your assurance that everything you have worked for all your life will be distributed to your loved ones, according to your wishes.

Planning Your Estate

Estate planning is not just for the wealthy. It is for anybody who wants to make sure their assets are handled properly and distributed to specific people (e.g., family members, friends, charities) in a predetermined way. If you do not create a formal transfer plan, your estate will be managed by the state and the courts a lengthy and expensive process that more often than not leads to undesirable outcomes.

An estate plan arranges the distribution of assets in your estate when you died and, if you become incapacitated, it can be used to make your wishes known in regards to your finances and personal care. Most estate planning begins with a will, which specifies who gets your property when you die. A living will is a supplemental document to a will. It allows you to spell out the medical treatment you want under specific circumstances. For example, you can specify whether you want life-support equipment under certain medical conditions so that your family members don't have to make the difficult decision on your behalf.

Before you start drafting estate-planning documents, such as a will, you need to know what you want to accomplish with your plan. Naming the right people or institutions to carry out your wishes is essential to any estate plan. If you don't name someone, a judge will decide who will be responsible for administering the distribution of your estate after you die. If you need assistance in setting up your estate plan, contact a qualified estate-planning attorney. Ask your friends or colleagues for a referral. The National Network of Estate Planning Attorneys is available on the Internet at *www.nnepa.com.*

For starters, never underestimate what your estate is worth. Many people get caught up with the routine of just trying to make a living and struggling to pay the bills to the point where they grossly underestimate the size of their estates. As a result, they fail to take appropriate tax-saving steps. Taxable estates include home equity, retirement-account balances, life insurance proceeds, securities, and foreign assets. Make sure you know your true worth and assess it accordingly in your estate.

Wills

Everybody needs a will, whether you are single or married, young or old, healthy or sick. By organizing your estate in a will to your best advantage, you can ensure that your hard-earned money stays in the family or goes to the people and organizations of your choice. In most states, if you die without a will, your estate is passed through a prolonged and expensive process called probate. And if you fail to properly prepare for estate taxes, your estate could end up getting taxed at rates that may exceed 50 percent.

If you die without a will, the court takes over and, in effect, writes a will for you in accordance with the state's intestacy laws. You can rest assured that when the courts get done with your will, none of it will look like what you would have wanted. The court appoints an administrator for your estate and a guardian for your children if one is needed.

A will instructs your survivors about how to distribute your property; it also enables you to nominate a guardian to care for your children should they become orphaned. You designate someone whom you trust to act as your estate's executor (e.g., your spouse), the person who will be responsible for taking inventory of your property, paying off your creditors and taxes, and ultimately splitting your estate among your heirs in accordance with the wishes you document in your will. Issues to consider in your will are summarized as follow:

State laws: Be careful that you do not bequeath property to heirs in a way that conflicts with state laws. Every state has laws that protect the interest of the spouse. In some states, a surviving spouse can claim as much as half of the estate, regardless of what you decree in your will.

Children: You should specifically mention your children and close relatives by name in the will, even if you choose not to leave them anything. This covers you in case there is a question later that their omission was a result of an oversight or mistake.

Allocation: Whenever possible, bequeath money in *percentages* rather than dollars. For example, if you own a mutual fund that is worth $100,000 today, its dollar value will fluctuate with market conditions. If your intent is to leave half of the fund to a niece, specify that your niece, by name, gets 50 percent of XYZ Fund.

Previous wills: After you have drafted a will, destroy any previous wills and be sure you include the phrase, "I revoke all prior wills and declare this my last will and testament." File a copy of your will with your other important papers and make sure that key people know how to access it should something happen to you. Review your will when major changes occur in your life, such as divorce, marriage, birth of children, or relocation to another state.

Living Trusts

Both wills and living trusts let you leave your property to the people you want to inherit it. You can revoke or change a will or a trust at any time, for any reason, before you die. The big difference between them is that assets left in a living trust don't have to go through probate court proceedings at your death. That's because when you create a living trust, you transfer ownership of the designated property to yourself as "trustee" of the trust. During your lifetime, you still have control over all the property in your living trust and can do what you want with it, sell it, spend it, or give it away. Then, after your death, the person you named in the trust to take over as trustee distributes the property to the family and friends you named.

A living trust involves more paperwork to create than a will because you must transfer ownership of the property to yourself as trustee and conduct future personal business in the name of the trust. But there is no need to file a separate tax return for the trust because all transactions, such as the sale of trust property at a profit, are reported on your personal income tax return. A trust also offers a way that the trust property can be taken care of if you become incapacitated and are unable to handle it yourself. The person you appointed in your trust to take over and manage your property does that for you. If you don't have a trust, close family members may have to go to court to get that kind of authority if you become incapacitated.

The bigger your estate, the bigger the potential probate cost and the less likely that your estate will qualify for simplified probate proceedings. Often it makes sense to making sure major assets, such as real estate or business assets are transferred in a way that avoids probate. You don't need a trust to avoid probate for assets like your 401(k) and other retirement accounts. It's a matter of filling out simple beneficiary forms that your 401(k) provider can give you.

A will can do one important thing that a living trust can't. It lets you name someone (called a personal guardian) to raise your minor children in the unlikely event that neither you nor the other parent is available. This is an important concern of most parents, who worry that their children will be left without a caretaker if they both die or are unavailable. State succession laws do not deal with the issue of who will take care of your children. If you don't name a guardian in your will, it is left up to the courts and social service agencies to find and appoint a personal guardian.

Wills Versus Trusts

Many people create both a will and living trust. It's common to use a living trust to leave some assets to heirs to avoid probate and leave the rest by will. In fact, even if you make a living trust, you'll still want to make a simple back-up will to handle property you didn't get around to transferring to the trust. Here are some factors to think about when you're deciding whether the centerpiece of your estate plan should be a will or a living trust:

What Wills and Trusts Can Do	Will	Trust
Avoid probate		X
Reduce estate tax	X	
Keep your estate plan confidential		X
Set up management of property for minors	X	X
Arrange management of your property if you become incapacitated		X
Appoint a guardian to raise young children if you can't	X	

Everybody should have a will and a living trust, whether you are single or married, young or old, healthy or sick. Making a will is the best way to leave property to family, friends and organizations of your choice after your death. By creating both documents, you are assured that your hard-earned money stays in the family or goes to the people or organization of your choice. You designate someone whom you have confidence in like your spouse or a sibling to act as your estate's executor. This person will be responsible for paying off your creditors and taxes, and ultimately splitting your estate among your heirs in accordance to the wishes you document in your will.

State laws determine whether a will or trust made by a resident of the state is valid. A will that is valid in the state where it is made is valid in all other states. Contrary to what many people believe a will or trust need not be notarized to be legally valid. But adding a notarized document to the document verifying that they were signed and witnessed can be helpful when it comes time to file the will in probate court.

If you decide to create a will or trust, consider using an estate-planning attorney to help you draft the documents. You can draft one from do-it-yourself personal computer software like Quicken's Will Maker (www.quicken.com), but any savings you incur over attorney fees are hardly worth the risk of a mistake or oversight on your part.

Preparing Wills and Trusts

When you create your will or trust, consider using an estate planning attorney to help draft your will. You can draft one from do-it-yourself software, but any savings you may incur are hardly worth the risk of a mistake or oversight. If you prefer to write the will or trust yourself, we caution you to do so only if your will is basic. Several software products can assist you with this process. The Learning Company offers a software product called Will Maker that is available at several computer stores and online at *www.nolo.com*. If you would like to read more about how a will works, pick up *Nolo's Simple Will Book* by Denis Clifford.

As a way to decide who gets your property, the will has been around in substantially the same form for about 150 years. Self-help was the rule and lawyer assistance was the exception. During the Civil War, it was highly unusual for a person to hire a lawyer to formally set out what should be done with his or her property. However, in the past 50 years, the legal profession has scored a public relations coup by convincing many people that writing a will without a lawyer is like doing your own brain surgery and you could make costly mistakes. The hardest part of making a will is figuring out who will get your property when you die.

In about half the states, handwritten wills called holographic wills, are legally valid. Most obvious problem with a holographic will is that after your death, it may be difficult to prove that your handwritten document was actually written by you and that you intended it to be your will. Only a few states accept oral wills under very limited circumstances, such as when a mortally injured person utters their last wishes. It is often difficult to prove the authenticity of an oral will. Handwritten wills or one that's prepared on your personal computer are fraught with possible legal problems as well. At a minimum, make sure you sign it and have it notarized.

A properly signed and witnessed will is much less vulnerable to challenge by anyone claiming it was forged or fabricated. If need be, witnesses can later testify in court that the person whose name is on the will is the same person who signed it, and that making the will was a voluntary and knowing act.

If you die without a valid will, money and other property you own at death will be divided and distributed to others according to your state's intestate succession laws. These laws divide all property among the relatives who are considered closest to you according to a set formula -- and completely exclude friends and charities.

Selecting Beneficiaries

When your spouse dies, your children if they are named as contingent beneficiaries would inherit your estate. If you're not married, or do not have children, you would name other beneficiaries. For example, if you designated your spouse as a primary beneficiary to inherit 75 percent and one of your kids to receive 25 percent, then you would have two primary beneficiaries. You could also designate multiple contingent beneficiaries each sharing whatever percentage you want.

You are allowed to name any beneficiary you want (i.e. person or organization) for a specified retirement account, and they get the money after you die. That's because retirement accounts are not controlled by the probate process and your will. If properly managed, this can work out great for your heirs. Beneficiaries are easy to make and change in your retirement accounts. You can do it online, by mailing a form that's provided by your trustee, or by direct contact with an authorized representative of the institution that administers your account.

You can make two types of beneficiary designations in an account: primary and contingent. The most common primary designation is with couples where the partner or spouse is named as the primary beneficiary and the kids or other family members are listed as contingent beneficiaries. For example, if your spouse is named as the primary, then when you die they would inherit the balance in your account. Usually, you cannot use a will or trust to leave certain kinds of assets, including:

- Bank accounts for which you have named a pay-on-death beneficiary

- Life insurance proceeds (they go to the beneficiary you named in the policy)

- Stocks and bonds for which you have named a transfer-on-death beneficiary

Property owned as "community property with the right of survivorship," automatically goes to the survivor when one of the co-owners dies. Property owned in joint tenancy automatically goes to the surviving spouse when you die. Individual retirement accounts, 401(k) plans, and certain pension funds go to the beneficiary you named in forms provided by the account custodian.

If you created your will with the help of an attorney, they will make sure you have properly designated your beneficiaries using the correct wording. You need to include their full name, date of birth, and Social Security number. If your accounts are under the name of a trust, you include the name of the trust, the date you created it, and its tax identification number or your Social Security number.

Power of Attorney Directives

A power of attorney directive ensures that someone you trust will be on hand to manage the many practical, financial tasks that will arise if you become incapacitated. For example, bills must be paid, bank deposits must be made and someone must handle insurance and benefits paperwork. Many other matters may need attention as well, from property repairs to managing investments or a small business. In most cases, a durable power of attorney for finances is the best way to take care of tasks like these. It's a good idea for everyone to have a power of attorney directive for finances and health-related issues named in their estate plan.

They're particularly important if you fear that health problems may make it impossible for you to handle your financial matters. It's vitally important that those close to you understand the kind of medical treatment you would or would not want if you were unable to speak for yourself. The person you name can also make other necessary health care decisions for you if you are too ill or injured to direct your own care. Depending on where you live, you may get a durable power of attorney advance health care directive or a durable power of attorney for health care.

Estate Taxes

Estate tax is not a concern for most people. The tax is levied on the property you own at your death, but a large amount of property is exempt from taxation. In 2009, that amount was $3.5 million, which means that most people don't need to worry about estate tax. If you're married, estate tax won't be an issue until the second spouse dies. When the first spouse dies, everything left to the surviving spouse is tax free. If the second spouse owns all the property and it's worth more than the estate tax exemption, estate tax will be due. If that's the case, it's worth doing some tax planning.

For most families, probate is a waste of time and money. It typically takes from nine to 18 months to file a deceased person's will with the court, gather the assets, pay debts, and eventually distribute what is left as the will directs. Fees for attorneys, appraisers, accountants and probate court can reduce by about 5 percent the amount left for survivors to inherit. Unless relatives are fighting over who gets what, or there are big claims against the estate, a court-supervised process is seldom necessary.

Protecting Your Estate with Insurance

The average American's wealth hits a peak during the start of their retirement. Therefore, properly covering your wealth and associated assets when you retire. It is also critical that you review your health and medical insurance closely at this stage in your life. You may be able to reduce some of your insurance plans and need to ramp up others. A single sickness or accident could cost everything you own and wipe out years of responsible financial planning. The following questions will help you prepare for the future, understand many aspects of insurance, and position yourself for full coverage through your retirement.

Most of us don't really know how much insurance we need. As a result, we tend to over insure ourselves in insignificant areas and underinsure ourselves in significant areas. If you don't know what you are doing when you buy insurance, you will ultimately get hurt. Understanding what deductibles are reasonable for you to pay is an important factor that you should review. For assistance, go to *www.smartmoney.com.The* site offers worksheets to help you determine how much insurance you need.

An insurance deductible is what you will pay, out of pocket, before you collect the balance due to you by your insurance provider. For example, if you have a $100 deductible on your health care plan, then you will be responsible for paying the first $100 before your insurance will begin to pay for the rest of your care. You can use deductibles to your advantage because the higher the deductible, the less the insurance plan will cost you. Also, you can often deduct these from your taxes. This can give you some breathing room when it comes to health care costs. For example, if you get a minimal deductible, such as $100, then you will pay more each month than a plan with, say, a $1,000 deductible.

Insurance companies are regulated by state governments. Call your state's insurance office and ask them to send you a rate comparison. Don't over or underinsure. For example, if your house is worth $100,000 and you insure it for $200,000 and it gets destroyed by fire, the most you'll get is $100,000. By the same token, don't underinsure your home. If your house is worth $100,000 and you insure it for $50,000, you'll only get $50,000 if it is destroyed.

One of the biggest opportunities you have to save money on your homeowner's policy, without taking on significant risks, is in the personal property part of your policy. Homeowner's policies do carry a deductible. The deductible could range anywhere from $0 to $1,000, or more. Here's how personal property liability and associated deductibles work. Generally speaking, personal property in and around your home is covered from perils such as fire and theft by your homeowner's policy. Most good homeowner's policies also cover your personal property when you're away from home, such as a camera that's stolen out of your car.

Make sure you shop different insurance companies for the best homeowner's rates. Prices can easily vary by 25 percent or more, depending on the company. For example, if one company is experiencing unusually high claim rates, they will simply increase their rates to all their holders.

Often you can experience a discount in the cost of insurance when you buy all of your insurance from one company. Purchasing your home, car, and health insurance from one provider can save you hundreds of dollars. It is worth getting several quotes from reputable companies and inquiring about combining all of your insurance under their umbrellas. Once you have their quotes, then compare the quotes and deductibles to find the best rates.

Most homes are insured with a homeowner's policy that combines property insurance and personal liability insurance. Your property insurance covers your home, its furnishings, and your personal belongings. If your home was destroyed by a fire, for example, you would have to spend a considerable amount of money to replace your furnishings. Personal liability insurance covers individuals or members of a household against claims from third parties. Mortgage lenders require homeowner's insurance on a house before they will approve a loan.

Life Insurance

Like auto insurance or homeowner's insurance, term insurance buys you pure protection. Its sole function is to provide financial support to your family or people you care about if you die. As is the case with any life insurance, the price increases as you get older. If you try to buy term insurance when you are in your sixties, you probably won't want to pay the "expensive" premiums. That's okay as long as you have built up sufficient savings to cover your spouse if something should happen to you and if all of your dependents are grown. On the surface, term insurance would seem to be much more preferable than whole life since it is considerably cheaper. However, whole life insurance policies come packaged with savings accounts.

Term policies end in a specified number of years, such as ten or twenty years. If you still need insurance coverage when your term policy runs out, you can always renew it if you're in good health. If you develop bad health conditions such as high blood pressure, you may be uninsurable, which is a major disadvantage of term insurance.

Whole life insurance remains in effect for the rest of your life, regardless of your physical condition. Whole life insurance, which is sometimes called cash value insurance or permanent life insurance, is expensive, but it offers several benefits over term life that are worth considering. For example, whole life insurance offers death benefits. This means that you get at least some of, and often much more than, the amount you spent on your premium.

Another benefit is that the premiums typically stay the same throughout the terms of the policy. Finally, if you are a conservative investor and have difficulty saving, traditional whole life insurance makes sense because it acts as a "savings account."These policies come packaged with all kinds of different features that are unique to each company offering them.

Whole life covers you with life insurance for your entire life. At some point, you will die and your whole life benefit will pay off. As we mentioned earlier, these policies accumulate a cash value over time. It usually takes at least five years before you will begin to build up cash value in your account. If you keep the policy long enough, your annual cash value can exceed the premium payment because of compound interest.

Insurance agents will be quick to tell you that over time, the life insurance part of your whole life policy costs you nothing because the cash in your account is generating enough interest to pay the annual premium. That's not true because the earned interest is *your* money that's paying the premium. Premiums for whole life typically remain the same over the life of the policy unless you pick one that has graduated premium rates.

Term insurance is great if you need a lot of cheap life insurance coverage over a specified number of years and you can simultaneously replace the protection it provides by building your investment portfolio. For example, if you have a health problem, you may want to carry additional life insurance now to cover your spouse while you settle your retirement. Whole life insurance policies are great if you want to have life insurance protection when you are in your seventies or eighties and need something that will force you to save money each month through monthly insurance payments. As mentioned previously, most whole life policies build up a cash value over time.

Like your retirement plan, an insurance plan should cover your financial needs in the event that your death adversely affects your loved ones financially. If you're married and living off two incomes, you and your spouse need to address the financial ramifications of one of you dying prematurely. Could the surviving spouse sustain your joint financial commitments (such as a mortgage, car payments, debt and loan payments) on a single income?

How do you determine how much life insurance you really need? One approach would be to multiply your combined incomes by the number of years your children will be dependents in order to get an estimate. For example, let's assume that you and your spouse have a combined annual income of $75,000. You have two children, ages

15 and 17, who you have decided will remain dependents until they reach the age of 21. The amount of life insurance coverage could be calculated as follows:

Coverage = (Combined Incomes x Dependent Years Remaining/Number of Dependents)

So using our example from above: Coverage would be $375,000.
Each spouse would need to purchase a life insurance policy equal to one half of the total amount needed (in this example, $375,000 or $187,500) to be able to cover the lost income if one of them were to die. In our example, we arbitrarily assumed that each spouse earns the same amount of money, or $37,500 after taxes a year, to simplify our illustration. If one spouse is earning more than the other spouse, the insurance coverage on the higher wage earner would be prorated. In either event, the calculated amount of insurance would be sufficient to cover the lost income should either spouse die before the kids become independent at age 21.

In its simplest form, you buy a life insurance policy that will pay your designated beneficiaries a specific amount of money if you die. Listen to the options your agent pitches to you, but don't lose focus on what you truly need. Shop around. When you shop for life insurance, contact at least two companies that you can negotiate with at the same time. All of them have different life products to offer at widely varying fees. Establish a baseline. In the interest of keeping it simple, get a price for a plain-vanilla term life policy in the amount that you need. It is the cheapest form of life insurance offered. You buy a specified amount of coverage (e.g., $100,000) for a term of years (e.g., 5 years). At the end of the term, the policy expires. It's as simple as that.

Your Estate Plan

An estate plan arranges for the distribution of assets in your estate when you die or if you are incapacitated. Most estate plans begin with a will, which specifies who gets your property when you die. A will combined with a living trust allows you to spell out what you want under specific circumstances. A will lets you name a personal guardian to raise your minor children if they are orphaned. Individual state laws determine whether a will or trust made by a resident is valid. Durable power of attorney is particularly important in the event that health problems make it impossible for you to handle your financial matters. Your estate plan is the final component in your retirement plan. It's your assurance that everything you have worked for all your life will be distributed to your loved ones, according to your wishes.

Chapter 10

Putting Everything Together

If all the parts fit when you put it together, the thing will work

All of us would like to be financially independent. To get there, many people try any get-rich-quick scheme that comes along, including the lottery. They'll invest in whatever somebody tells them is a ground-floor opportunity to make it happen. Others will adopt a more scientific approach and, with all good intentions, seek out the advice of an investment broker and invest in something without much thought.

Even though we may try completely different investment approaches, most of us share two common failings: our retirement plans are not consistent, and if we managed to set goals, we will not follow them to achieve the financial security we want. As a result, many people will move into their retirement years subsisting on substandard retirement incomes. We caution you to be realistic when you create your retirement plan and follow the guidelines we have given you to achieve the financial independence you seek in order to retire.

Retirement planning is the process you go though to develop a financial plan that will cover you during your retirement years. We've addressed well over a hundred retirement planning issues in the previous chapters. It's now time to consolidate everything you've learned into a simple retirement plan. If you start with a financial plan, a solid set of financial goals, and work out from there, you will become financially independent. If you already have a retirement plan in place, great! If you don't, then start one today. If you are fortunate enough to own a home, a retirement plan combined with a home that's paid off are two of the most important steps you can take to secure your financial future. The rest is up to you.

In the old days, retirement planning was simple. Once you turned 65, you collected social security and an employer pension, moved to Florida, and lived happily ever after. Well, not anymore! With time, that has all changed. Many people want to retire early; many others want to work longer. Guaranteed pensions are disappearing and are being replaced with self-directed retirement plans. As a result, retirement planning has become more complex and more important.

At a time when employers are dropping guaranteed pensions and social security is struggling to meet the increased financial demands of the retiring baby boomers, what's a person to do? Take a proactive approach and develop the best retirement plan you can that meets your exact expectations and any potential future problems.

A well coordinated retirement plan will help you get through a time of your life when, financially, you are probably going to be living on less than you're used to. Retirement planning incorporates a multitude of sub-plans to assure that your happiness and financial well-being are maintained during your retirement years. People who choose not to take the time to develop a retirement plan usually end up not knowing where they've been, and they have no idea where they're going.

Your plan should include a wide variety of things. To find out the contents of a plan, consider reviewing an existing tool that is created to help you with your planning process. For example, Fidelity Investments offers several excellent retirement planning tools on their website *(www.fidelity.com)*. Click on the "Retirement and Guidance" option that appears in the upper center section of Fidelity's main menu to get started. All legal documents and any material that is pertinent to your plan should be included in your retirement plan folder such as:

Savings plan. A monthly plan that shows what you have currently saved and what you plan to save throughout your retirement years. It helps to show where you are financially and where you are planning to be throughout your retirement years.

Insurance policies. Including these documents makes it much easier on whoever has to follow up on this information in the future. For example, if you are a widow and you supply your retirement plan to your only daughter, you have a vested interest in making sure she has all the information she may need one day. If you were to become seriously ill, she would most likely need to step in and assist by following up on your insurance policies. Therefore, keeping her or anyone else you choose current on your insurance status is critical.

Investment portfolio. This goes along with what was said about your insurance policies. Keep your plan as financially current as you can. Situations can change and you want to make sure that your trusted person (possibly the holder of your power of attorney if something were to happen to you) has all of your investment information so that she can engage as needed.

Fidelity Investments offers a service that's free even if you are not a Fidelity client. It's called the Fidelity Retirement Income Advantage and it is designed for people within ten years of retirement. One of their financial planners will create a comprehensive retirement income plan, including a withdrawal strategy, to help you meet expenses. Charles Schwab also offers free support; you can get more information at *www.schwab.com.* Check with your main financial resources or favorite financial institution to see what expert advice they offer to their clients. There are several good professionals who can help you create and refine your retirement plan:

See a *certified financial planner* to obtain an objective opinion and overview of your retirement plan.

See a *certified public accountant (CPA)* for tax planning, budget planning, personal business advice, and retirement income projections.

See an *insurance agent* for a review of the insurance policies that you may or may not need to supplement your retirement plan.

See a *securities broker* to set up an IRA or a 401(k) plan or to buy securities on your behalf to augment your retirement plan.

See a *trust attorney* to set up a will or living trust to protect your loved ones in your plan.

It is always a good idea to give backup copies of your retirement plan to trusted individuals. This may include people who are written into your plan, such as your children or siblings. To answer this question correctly, just think about who would need to have a copy of your plan in case something happened to you. Then make sure that those individuals have copies or know where to find a copy as needed.

Appendix A

Glossary of Terms

401(k) plan is a broad label for a variety of employer-sponsored retirement savings incentive programs.

403(b) plan is a retirement plan available to employees of public schools, nonprofit organizations, or the clergy. It is identical to the 401(k), except that employers need not contribute, and they aren't subject to 401(k)'s stringent Employee Retirement Income Security Act (ERISA).

457 deferred-compensation plan sometimes called a deferred-camp plan, this retirement plan defers an employee's pay by the amount contributed, a characteristic shared by 401(k) and SIMPLE plans.

Account aggregator is an online platform that presents data from multiple accounts in a single interface that stores log-in information and simplifies web access to personal financial information.

Accrual method is an accounting method often used by businesses with inventory; with this method, you report income and deduct expenses when the work's done (you've done all the things you have to do to get paid and all the expenses have been incurred).

Active management is an investment management style that presumes that investments guided by a fund manager and informed by industry and economic insight should perform better than other similar investments.

Adjusted gross income (AGI) is the amount of income calculated by adding work income and other income such as investment interest and dividends or alimony. It excludes such things as alimony paid and the cost of health insurance paid by the self-employed.

Administrative fees are the fees that cover the cost of running the plan itself, including expenses such as the cost of preparing annual reports, running required discrimination tests, and supporting the website and customer service department.

Advertising is a means of informing the public about your product or service.

After-tax contributions are contributions to an IRA that is not deductible from a filer's tax obligation.

Age Discrimination in Employment Act was passed in 1967 and prohibits any employer from refusing to hire, discharge, or discriminate in any way based on a person's age.

Alternative minimum tax was created to close loopholes that enabled some super-rich taxpayers to pay unfairly low or even no taxes by resorting to legal tax shelters. Unfortunately, the tax lacks indexes to inflation, making more middle-class families vulnerable to assessment.

Angels are private investors willing to lend money or equity capital in much the same way as venture capitalists, but on a much smaller scale.

Annual expense ratio is the percentage of plan assets that are paid to cover operating, management, and marketing costs.

Annuity is a financial contract. You buy an annuity with the guarantee that the company-usually an insurance company-will provide a series of regular, fixed payments in exchange. Annuities come in a variety of forms.

Asset allocation is an investment recipe for all an individual's accounts, dictating the percentage of a portfolio invested in stocks, bonds, or cash.

Assisted living is a kind of housing that provides a modest amount of assistance, including bathing, dressing, and cooking meals.

Baby boomers are people born in a flourish of family-boosting activity that followed World War II and continued into the 1960s.

Balance sheet is a listing of assets, liabilities, and an owner's investment in a business as of a fixed date, such as the end of a quarter or year.

Basis is the amount you paid for property (called cost basis) or other amount treated as your investment in property. Adjusted basis is basis increased by additions or improvements and decreased by depreciation.

Benchmark is a standard used to compare performance, such as the Standard and Poor's 500 Index.

Blog is a web log that can be a marketing tool to express your political gripes, position you as an expert, and draw interest to your website.

Board and care is a type of assisted living that generally offers group meals and other activities for residents who want to spend time with friends and neighbors.

Bonds are a form of loan. In buying a bond, you're effectively entering into a contract with the issuer of that bond to pay whatever money you invested, plus interest. Bonds come in a variety of forms.

Book value is the real value of a company. It's calculated by totaling all assets and subtracting debt and liabilities.

Broadband service is a technology that allows the Internet connection to your computer to run faster and better.

Brochure ware is a website that functions like a written brochure, listing your product or services, rates, and contact information.

Business opportunity is a non-franchise arrangement in which you buy a concept for a product or service.

Business plan is a written report describing what a business is all about and where the business is heading in the future.

C Corporation is organized under state law and taxed as a separate person, but treated as a regular corporation.

Call provision are bonds that are paid off prior to their prearranged maturity.

Capital gain tax rate is the percentage of investing profits that must be paid in taxes, calculated as a proportion of the profit or capital gain of an investment.

Career average plans are similar to final pay programs, but based on the average of all the years you work for a company. You may get a percentage of your salary for every year you were in the plan. In other cases, you may get an average for all years you were in the plan.

Cash flow cycle time is the time over which inventory is ordered, paid for, sold, and the money is received.

Cash method is an accounting method often used by service businesses. With this method, you record income when your client pays you and deduct expenses as they come up.

Cash value life insurance is a form of life insurance that builds accompanying cash value. These come in several different forms.

Catastrophic coverage is health insurance with exceedingly high deductibles.

Certificates of Deposits (CDs) are a form of promissory note; the lender effectively promises to pay you a certain interest rate if you let them hold your money for a specified amount of time.

COBRA (Consolidated Omnibus Budget Reconciliation Act) requires companies with 20 or more employees to allow you to stay on your health plan for an additional 18 months after you leave your job.

Cohousing is a semi-communal living arrangement where separate living units are arranged around a "common house."

Compounding is the effect of money earning interest which, in turn, results in a larger sum that earns even more.

Congregate housing is a variant of assisted living, offering both a level of assisted care as well as private living space.

Continuing care retirement communities involves several types of housing and living arrangements, including independent living facilities, assisted living, and nursing homes. Retirees can remain in the same retirement community, with the option to change the level of care they receive as their individual needs mandate it.

Conventional IRA was the first Individual Retirement Account introduced and defers any tax impact until you begin to withdraw money from the account.

Custodian is the institution that holds your IRA. It can be a bank, brokerage house, or similar place.

Certificate of deposit is a bank's promissory note to repay the amount deposited, with interest, at a future date, typically one month to five years away.

Chat rooms are locations on the Internet in which people interact with each other on a particular topic or area of mutual interest.

Cliff vesting is a vesting schedule in which none of an employer's contribution becomes an asset of the employee until the employee reaches a specified work anniversary. At the anniversary date, the employer's full contribution belongs to the employee.

Closely held corporation is a privately owned corporation whose stock is not traded on any public exchange.

Collection agency is a business that performs collection services, including sending reminders to late payers and suing delinquents on your behalf.

Commercial loan is money borrowed from a bank or other financial institution that specializes in business lending.

Compound interest is an investment principal in which interest is paid not only on the principal saved but also on the accumulated interest from prior periods that has not been withdrawn.

Constructive receipt is the date when income is treated as having been received by cash-basis businesses because it's under their control, even if they don't actually have the cash in hand (a check is income when received even though you haven't deposited or cashed it yet).

Contribution is an amount of cash or other assets deposited in a retirement account.

Cost of goods sold is the cost of inventory items such as materials, labor, and packaging.

Debt is borrowed money for financing a business. The borrower is called the debtor; the lender is called the creditor.

Deductible for insurance purposes is the amount of damage or liability that the insurance company won't cover. For taxes, it's the amount of expenses you can subtract against income.

Deep discount broker is an investment house that sells stocks and funds very inexpensively.

Defined benefit program is a pension payout based on your salary and number of years of service.

Defined contribution program is a program in which money is automatically deducted from your salary before you take possession of it. From there, the money is put into an investment vehicle of your choosing, including mutual funds, company stock, and other options.

Depreciation is a deduction of a portion of the cost of a car or other equipment you own over the life of the equipment (the life is set by the IRS) to reflect its true value.

Direct rollover is a process that directly transfers assets from one retirement plan into another.

Disability insurance provides income if you become disabled or temporarily unable to earn a living.

Discount brokers charge less than full-service brokers to execute trades.

Dividends are payments to shareholders authorized by a company's board of directors. They can be in cash or additional shares of the company's stock.

Dollar cost averaging is a savings strategy involving investing the same dollar amount at fixed intervals. If share prices increase, fewer shares are bought or if they decrease, more shares are bought at the different intervals.

Domain name is the address n the Internet where people can find your website.

Dow Jones Industrials is a stock index made up of 30 of the largest publicly held companies traded on the New York Stock Exchange.

Dying intestate is the legal term that refers to lack of a will or trust that provides instructions after someone dies.

ECHO is an acronym for Elder Cottage Housing Opportunities. This is usually a separate, small manufactured home that is added onto the side or backyard of an existing home.

Employee stock ownership plan (ESOP) is a program that allows employees to buy company stock, often with little or no commission.

Employer identification number is the number assigned to a business owner by the IRS after you file IRS Form SS-4. This is used for identification purposes on tax returns, bank accounts, and retirement plans.

Endorsement is a correction or change to an existing insurance policy.

Entrepreneur is someone who organizes and directs a start-up business, assuming the risk in the hope of making a profit.

Equity is the value of your home after subtracting the mortgage balance.

Equity financing a business happens when you bring investors in as part owners of the business.

Escrow is an arrangement in which a third party holds funds; when certain conditions are met, the funds are paid out.

Exchange traded funds (ETFs) are pooled investment accounts that resemble mutual funds in that they hold a basket of many individual investments but are traded directly on the stock exchanges by investors buying and selling their shares like stocks.

Expense ratio takes in all expenses incurred by a fund's operations and expresses them in terms of percentages.

Face value is the principal; the amount of money you invested when you bought a bond. It's also known as par value.

Fair market value is what a willing buyer and willing seller would pay, if neither is being forced to buy or sell and each understands all the facts and circumstances of the deal.

Fee for service is a form of health insurance that lets you choose any doctor or health care provider you like. Generally, the coverage pays 80 percent of any costs you accumulate.
You are obligated to pick up the remaining 20 percent.

Fee-only financial planner is a financial advisor who charges only for his advice, based on the consultation duration or project scope, and who doesn't sell investment products for commission in order to avoid conflict of interest in investment choice recommendations.

FICA (Federal Insurance Contributions Act) is the Social Security and Medicare taxes on wages paid by both the employer and the employee.

Final pay plan is a pension that can offer the biggest payout, as they average your salary over the last several years you're employed at a company.

Financial statement is information about income, expenses, sales figures, and other number-oriented items such as a cash flow statement, balance sheet, or profit and loss statement.

Fixed annuity is a tax deferred financial instrument marketed by insurance companies and brokerage firms that pays a fixed rate of interest that readjusts annually. Fixed Annuities are similar to CDs in that they pay a fixed rate of interest that readjusts on a yearly basis. Annuities are sold by life insurance companies and some brokerage firms.

Flat benefit plan is one of the most simple and straightforward pension payout. You receive a set monthly amount based on how long you worked for a company.

Flexible spending account is a program that allows you to set aside money from your salary tax-free. These funds can then be used to

117

help pay for medical expenses that are not covered by your employer's health plan.

Franchise is a business arrangement that gives you the right to sell a product or service in a particular area. The company selling the concept is the franchisor; you are the franchisee. The right to a large territory is called a master franchise.

Fulfillment company is a business that takes and processes orders for you, including acceptance of payment by credit card. Generally, a fulfillment company charges a flat fee.

Full retirement age is the age at which you can receive your full retirement benefit from Social Security.

Fund family is several different mutual funds that a company maintains and offers to clients. The funds are usually set up for different financial objectives.

Fundamental analysis is a stock analysis involving examination of a company's operating statistics and numbers.

FUTA (Federal Unemployment Tax Act) is the Federal unemployment insurance tax paid by an employer on an employee's wages.

Goodwill is a favorable reputation of a business, which is considered an intangible asset.

Graded vesting is a vesting schedule in which an employer's contribution vests gradually over time, in stages or grades.

Grants are money from government sources or private foundations to start or run a business that matches the goals of the grant maker; grant money doesn't have to be repaid. .

Gross income is income before deductions. For purposes of the home office deduction, gross income means money from business minus expenses that don't relate to the use of the home such as office supplies or the salary of an employee.

Guaranteed investment contracts (GICs) is a contract involving a guaranteed rate of return.

Hobby loss rules are the tax rules that prevent an individual from deducting business expenses that are greater than business income where there's no reasonable expectation of making a profit from the business.

Home equity line of credit is a loan secured by the amount of equity you have in your home.

Home-office deduction is the total of deductions from the business use of a home office, including depreciation on the office or a portion of rent, as well as the portion of utilities and insurance related to the home office.

HTML (Hypertext Markup Language) is the programming language used on computers to create websites.

Independent contractor is a person who contracts to provide work according to his own methods. This person isn't under the control of the person or business for which the work is being performed (not an employee).

Income tax rate is the percentage of one's income that must be paid to local, state, or federal government.

Individual retirement accounts (IRA) are planned accounts that carry a tax advantage intended to encourage savings.

Individual 401(k) is a retirement savings program best suited for someone who works on their own and has no plans to bring on any employees in the future.

Inflation is the effect of rising prices on the value of money to buy goods and services.

Irrevocable trust is a trust that can't be changed in any way during the grantor's lifetime.

Internet is a worldwide collection of computer networks that you can access with a computer, modem, telephone line, and an online service provider or Internet service provider.

Invoice is an itemized list of products you've sold to someone, stating the quantity, price, and terms of sale; a bill for services rendered.

IRA basis is the amount contributed to an IRA that isn't eligible for tax deduction.

IRA trustee fees are costs paid by the investor that can include sales commissions, management fees, and marketing fee.

Joint and several liabilities is a legal rule that makes two or more parties fully responsible for damages, debt repayment, and other legal obligations.

Keogh plan is a tax-deferred retirement plan that lets small business owners and the self-employed save money for retirement.

Lifestyle funds are investment pools that resemble target-date funds in that they are a mix of mutual funds in an asset allocation that the mutual fund company chooses but that cater to risk tolerances.

Limited liability company is a type of business organization formed under state law that gives owners protection from personal liability but treats them as a partnership for tax purposes.

Limited partnership is a partnership in which one or more partners has limited personal liability and can't participate in the day-to-day operations of the business.

Limit orders is a stock purchase system that lets you establish prices at which you wish to buy or sell.

Living will also known as an advanced medical directive, this is a document that outlines your decisions about any sort of life-sustaining treatment.

Long-term care insurance is insurance you buy to pay for nursing home care and other sorts of long-term, comprehensive care.

Managed care also known as health maintenance organizations, is less expensive than fee for service. However, you have a limited choice of health care providers.

Medicaid is the federal program designed to pay for health care for the poor.

Medicare is the federal medical care program for persons age 65 and up. It is subdivided into four parts, offering different forms of coverage.

Medigap insurance is supplemental insurance to cover any gaps in Medicare coverage.

Marginal tax rate is the rate on the highest bracket a taxpayer's income reached.

Marketing is how people advertise, publicize, or otherwise inform each other of their product or service with the goal of exchanging products or services with each other.

Matching contribution is the employer plan-match option under which an employer promises to match a certain percentage of each employee's contribution up to a specific percentage of their pay.

Medical IRA known as a health savings account is an individual retirement account in which account holders can deposit pretax money to pay for medical expenses.

Modified adjusted gross income known as modified AGI, is the adjusted gross income from an IRA withdrawal by someone age

591/2 or older, disabled or deceased, using the withdrawals to pay for college or other qualified higher education expenses, or using withdrawals toward a first-time home purchase.

Money market deposit account is an investment account that often pays lower interest than a CD, but whose assets are accessible anytime without waiting for a future maturity date.

Money market fund is an investment account whose the cash in the account is accessible at anytime.

Monte Carlo calculator is a calculator that generates a measure of the probability that a given investment outcome scenario will result in a financially comfortable retirement based on expected assets, probable lifetime, and economic conditions.

Mutual funds are a combination of individual investments such as stocks, bonds, and cash bundled together into one product.

Net operating losses are business expenses in excess of business income; business losses that can be carried back 2 years and forward 20 years; also called NOLs.

Net unrealized appreciation is the difference in value between the average cost that you paid for stock and its current market value.

Network marketing is direct sales to consumers with distributors getting money from both direct sales and a percentage of the direct sales of other distributors they bring into the network.

Networking is word-of-mouth marketing in which contacts are made to try to drum up business.

Nonretirement accounts are bank or mutual fund accounts that are not held inside IRAs and on which taxes must be paid as accrued.

Overhead is the cost of monthly expenses, including electricity, telephone, insurance, and salaries of employees.

Partnership occurs when two or more people working together in a business with the intention of making a profit.

Passive management is an investment management style that seeks to match the market's performance.

Personal service corporation is subject to special tax rules; corporation engaged in the fields of health, law, accounting, engineering, architecture, actuarial science, performing arts, or consulting that meets certain ownership and service tests.

Plan provider is the company hired by an employer to administer their retirement plan, who often acting as the plan's trustee as well.

Points represent an up-front interest payment to a lender. One point is equivalent to 1 percent of the amount borrowed.

Power of attorney allows someone to make decisions when you're incapable of doing so yourself. Examples include medical and financial power of attorney.

Pretax contribution to a tax deferred retirement amount that a filer is permitted to deduct from their tax obligation.

Price-earnings ratio (PIE) is a popular stock ratio that illustrates how much an investor would be willing to spend in return for $1 in company earnings.

Price/book ratio (PIB) is a ratio that compares a stock's price to what a company is worth.

Price/sales ratio (P/S) is ratio that is calculated by dividing a current stock price by a company's earnings per share.

Primary insurance amount (PIA) is all your Social Security cash benefits, including your monthly benefit as well as benefits for dependents and survivors.

Probate is the legal process that the state must go through should you die with property still in your name.

Prime rate is the interest rate banks charge their preferred customers.

Profit sharing contribution is an employer contribution to their employees' retirement account that is made based on the profits of the company.

Promotion is the act of stimulating an immediate sale with special offers, such as discount coupons.

Publicly held corporation issues stock that is traded on a public exchange such as the New York stock exchange.

QUADRO is a divorce-specific transfer between two people's accounts requiring a court order.

Qualified is a term that means a pension program has to adhere to certain governmental guidelines for tax purposes.

Real estate investment trusts (REITs) are funds that invest in property, including shopping centers, apartment buildings, and similar commercial operations.

Rebalancing are adjustments to an asset allocation that correct for different assets having performed differently over time, eventually comprising different portfolio percentages than intended.

Reverse mortgage is a mortgage that lets you tap the accumulated equity in your home. In doing so, your loan balance increases rather than going down.

Revocable trust is a trust that may be changed or eliminated completely.

Rider is an additional clause to an existing contract or insurance policy to cover a special item or event (usually an upgrade to a policy); sometimes referred to as an endorsement.

Risk tolerance is the amount of uncertainty and volatility with which an investor feels comfortable.

Roth 401(k) is an employer-sponsored retirement account in which tax liability accrues upon contribution but whose account earnings and withdrawals are tax-free.

Roth 403(b) is an employer-sponsored retirement account offered to employees of public schools, nonprofit organizations, and the clergy in which tax liability accrues upon contribution but whose account earnings and withdrawals are tax-free.

Roth IRA is a form of individual retirement account in which taxes do not accrue on withdrawn funds, whether earnings or basis.

S Corporation also called a Subchapter S Corporation is organized under state law that elects to have business income taxed to its shareholders.

Safe-harbor 401(k) is an employee-sponsored plan that reduces an employer's effort and cost in running the plan's nondiscrimination tests.

SBA (Small Business Administration) is a federal agency that sponsors loan programs and other assistance to small businesses.

SBICs (Small Business Investment Companies) are privately managed firms licensed by the SBA to make loans to small businesses.

Search engines are websites that enable you to find other pages on the web, just like a library card catalog helps you find books on shelves.

Self-employment tax is Social Security and Medicare taxes paid by self-employed individuals, such as sole proprietors, on their net earnings from the business.

Self-insured is having sufficient assets to make life insurance unnecessary.

SEP plan known as the Simplified Employee Pension plan is a retirement option popular with people who are self-employed and who don't have employees in which 100 percent of the contributions *come from the employer.

Shareholders are the owners of a corporation (also called stockholders) whose ownership interest is in the form of stock certificates.

Shares outstanding are the total number of shares owned by an investor.

SIMPLE 401(k) plan is a plan that combines the features of SIMPLE IRAs and regular 401(k) plans, including contribution limits and employer match rules of SIMPLE plans.

SIMPLE IRA is an acronym for Savings Incentive Match Plan. This type of IRA is particularly suited to someone whose self-employment income is relatively modest-$30,000 annually or less.

SIMPLE Plan also known as the Savings Incentive Match Plan for Employees is a common option in companies with 30 or fewer employees but available to companies with up to 100 employees, an IRA account into which both employee and employer can contribute.

Simplified Employee Pensions is retirement plan available to employers and the self-employed. All contributions are tax-deductible.

Single-person 401(k) also called a solo 401(k) and a self-employed 401(k) is a retirement plan that simplifies the administration of a 401(k) enough to make it affordable for single-person companies and very small enterprises.

Sixty-day rollover is a transfer of assets from a 401(k) plan to an individual retirement account during a 60-day period and that assesses a 10 percent early withdrawal penalty unless the rollover is not completed in 60 days.

Social Security formally known as the Federal Old Age, Survivors and Disability Insurance program provides retirement funding and other benefits to participants.

Sole proprietorship is an unincorporated business owned by one person.

Solution providers are companies that provide all-in-one packages for running an online business (usually for a flat monthly fee).

Start-up phase is the period in which a business begins operation, generally the first three months.

Stock is a share of ownership in a company. Stocks come in a variety of types, with different features and objectives.

Stop loss orders is a method of stock buying specifically designed to limit your losses and protect whatever profit you may have earned from a stock.

Summary Plan Description (SPD) is the book of rules that governs your specific 401(k) plan, including when an employee will be eligible to participate and the specifics about how to contribute to the account and how money can be withdrawn.

Surrender value is the amount you receive if you cash out a life insurance policy.

Target date fund is a mutual fund whose allocation of assets are tailored to perform best within a time specific event, like your retirement date.

Tax credit is a reduction in income tax on a dollar-for-dollar basis.

Tax deferred is the income gains generated by investments that do not become taxable until the funds are withdrawn from the account.

Tax-deductible is the quality of income or capital gains generated by investments that can reduce tax liability by the amount deposited into a retirement account.

Taxable income is the earning from an individual's job and investments that are taxable each year.

Teaser cards are credit cards with very low interest rates that last only for a limited amount of time.

Technical analysis is a stock analysis on which a company's trading patterns are charted and analyzed.

Term life insurance is the simplest form of life insurance, as it involves no cash value.

Testamentary trust is a trust, created under a last will and testament that becomes effective only after the grantor dies and the will is admitted to probate.

Timing the market means determining at a particular moment in time, which way the market is going – up or down or sideways.

Treasury securities are issued and backed by the federal government. They come in various forms, including securities, notes, savings bonds, and other formats.

Trustee fees are the cost paid by investors in retirement accounts that can include sales commissions, management, and administration fees.

Trusts are a legal vehicle in which one person (known as the trustee) holds property for another person (known as the beneficiary). This trustee can be a person or a trust company. Trusts are useful in distributing the assets of an estate.

Turnkey business is a business that is ready to go into operation, with all materials, processes, and equipment in place to produce a product or service.

Umbrella insurance is an additional form of liability insurance coverage.

Unearned income is income you don't earn. Common examples are pension and annuity payouts, dividends, and interest and proceeds from life insurance.

URL (Uniform Resource Locator) is another name for a web address.

Value averaging is a variant on dollar-cost averaging that takes into account stock price movement.

Variance is a change or alteration of a zoning rule granted specifically for one person.

Venture capitalists are people or companies that invest in businesses (often technology related) with the expectation of realizing big profits in the future.

Virtual workers are people who do jobs from their own locations, such as answering your telephone from their home offices rather than from your office.

Waiting period is the time between the onset of a disability and when benefits begin.

Will is a written document that delineates how you want your property distributed after you die.

Withdrawal is a cash value of an asset redeemed from a retirement account.

Work credits are a system to determine Social Security eligibility. You become formally eligible once you have accumulated 40 "work credits."

Yield is the effective rate of interest that a bond pays to investors.

Appendix B

Useful Information

Annual Reports

Investor Guide (*www.investorguide.com/stocklist.cgi*) provides links to thousands of publicly traded companies.

Best Calls (*www.bestcalls.com*) provides access to companies' quarterly earnings press conferences.

Public Register's Annual Report Service (*www.prars.com*) offers both online and hard copy annual reports.

Thomson Investor Net (*www.thomsoninvest.net*) covers more than 7,000 in-depth company reports that are updated twice a month.

Security Exchange Commission (SEC) is the official government site that hosts all financial reports of the publicly traded companies in the United States. The website is at *www.sec.gov*.

Bonds

Bonds Online (*www.bondsonline.com*) provides charts and historical data that compare the various bond market sectors.

The Bond Market (*www.bondcan.com*) specializes in investing in Canadian bonds.

The Bond Market Association (*www.bondmarket.com*) is loaded with information about thousands of bonds and their respective trading history.

Brokers

Charles Schwab (*www.schwab.com*)

Fidelity Investments *(www.jidelity.com)*

T. Rowe Price *(www.troweprice.com)*

Vanguard Group *(www.vanguard.com)*

Budgeting

You can view a sample budget at *www.personalbudgeting.com*. A good resource for developing a budget is available at *www.simpleplanning.net*. The following websites contain good budget tools:

www.flexibleretirementplanner.com
www.smartmoney.com
www.money.com
www.personalbudgeting.com
www.simpleplanning.com
www.tdameritrade.com
www.fidelity.com/myplan

Credit Cards and Credit Scores

To find out about credit card options, visit *www.e-wisdom.com*. The website at *www.cardratings.com* offers a variety of resources to help you understand everything related to credit cards. For a fee, you can find out what your score is at *www.myjico.com*. You can check your credit report at all three bureaus at *www .annualcreditreport.com*. The following websites will provide you with additional information about credit cards and credit scores:

www.cardrating.com
www.cardratings.com
www.myfico.com
www.annualcreditreport.com

Debt Reduction

If you need more advice on reducing your debt, try Barnes & Noble's website *www.barnesandnoble.com)* or Amazon's website *(www.amazon.com)* and browse through their debt-related books. The website at *http://cgi.money.cnn.com/tools/debtplanner/debtplannerjsp* will help you project when you will be debt free. If you are interested in learning more about bankruptcy, go to *www.banhruptcvinfo.com.* Qpicken.com offers a Debt Reduction Planner, an excellent tool for about $50. The following websites will provide you with debt reduction information:

www.defeatthedebt.com
www.cgi.money.cnn.com
www.bankrupcyinfo.com
www.smartmoney.com
www.money.com
www.simpleliving.net
www.debetorsanonymous.org
www.clearbankrupcy.com

Discount Brokers

Accutrade *(www.accutrade.com) 800-494-8939*

American Express (*www.americanexpress.com) 800-658-4677*

Morgan Stanley *(www.morganstanley.com) 212-761-4000*
E*Trade *(www.etrade.com) 800-387-2331*

Fidelity *(wwwjidelity.com) 800-544-8666*

Muriel Siebert *(www.msiebert.com) 800-872-0444*

Schwab *(www.schwab.com) 800-435-4000*

Scottrade *(scottrade.com) 800-619-7283*

Wall Street Access *(www.wsaccess.com) 800-925-5782*

TD Ameritrade *(www.tdameritrade.com) 800-669-3900*

Diversified Investing

Legg Mason's website *(www.leggmason.com)* provides an online questionnaire to help you develop a diversification plan.

Frank Russell Company' (*www.russell.com)* features a Comfort Quiz to help you allocate your investments.

Fidelity's Asset Diversification Planner *(www.fidelity.com)* offers diversification advice, a risk questionnaire, and model portfolios.

The Intelligent Asset Allocator *(www.eJficientfrontier.com)* offers comprehensive information on how to build a diversified portfolio.

Education

To learn more about federal financial aid for college and how to apply, visit the U.S. Department of Education's website at *www.ed.gov.*

The American Association of Individual Investors offers advice on funds and portfolio management on their website at *www.aaii.com.*

Bloomberg Personal Finance *(www.bloomberg.com)* offers online training when you click on the Bloomberg University module.

Investing Basics *(www.aaii.com/invbas)* offers feature articles about how to start successful investment programs, pick winning stocks, and evaluate your options.

Investor Guide (*www.investorguide.com*) features more than 1,000 answers to frequently asked questions.

Money 101 provides an interactive investment seminar at *www.money.cnn.com*. Money's *www.eldernet.comlmoney.htm* offers tutorials and advice on investing in stocks, mutual funds, and bonds.

Morningstar's University (*www.morningstar.com*) offers a comprehensive investment education program. The Motley Fools offer an investment seminar on their website at *www.fool.com*.

The Mutual Fund Education Alliance is the trade association for no-load funds and offers advice on how to select funds *(www.mfea.com).*

Vanguard *(www.vanguard.com)* offers online courses that cover the fundamentals of investing in mutual funds.

Estate Planning

If you want to create a basic will on your computer, Quicken offers a software product called Will Maker that is available in computer stores and at *www.nolo.com*. The following websites will provide you with additional estate planning information:

www.quicken.com
www.nolo.com
www.smartmoney.com
www.money.com
www.kinplinger.com
www.smartmoney.com/retirement
www.mpower.com
www.financialengines.com
www.morningstar.com

Financial Calculators

www.kinplinger.com

www.socialsecurity.gov/estimator
www.fincalc.com
www.dinkytown.com
www.calc.xml
www.dinkytown.com
www.riskgrades.com
www.choosetosave.org/calculators
www.schwab.com
www.troweprice.com/ric

Financial and Economic News

The Bureau of Economic Analysis *(www.bea.gov)* calculates economic indicators such as the gross domestic product and other regional, national, and international data, all of which are displayed on their website.

Census Bureau *(www. census.gov)* provides information about industry statistics and general business conditions.

STAT-USA *(www.stat-usa.gov)* is sponsored by the U.S. Department of Commerce and provides financial information about economic indicators, statistics, and economic news.

Financial Planning Organizations

The American Institute of Certified Public Accountants *(www.aicpa.org)*
Personal Financial Planning Division, 1211 Avenue of the Americas, New York, NY 10036, 800-862-4272

The National Association of Personal Financial Advisors *(www. nap/a. org)* 355 W. Dundee Rd., Suite 200, Buffalo Grove, IL 60089, 800-333-6659

A website that offers a variety of articles on financial planning is at *ww.money.cnn.com.*

Financial Publications and News Sites

www.money.cnn.com
www.cnnmoney.com
www.simpleplanning.com
www.fidelity.com
www.businessweek.com
www.kinplinger.com
www.morningstar.com
www.kiplinger.com
www.Yodlee.com
www.investools.com
www.quicken.com
www.fidelity.com
www.Smartinvestmentbook.com

Financial Tools

The Financial Center *(wwwfinancia!center.com)* has a section for retirees. Choose United States and then financial planning. Under this category, choose retirement. Schwab *(www.schwab.com)* helps you develop a financial plan with its online calculators, tools, and advice. Virtual Stock Exchange by Market Watch *(www.virtualstock exchange.com)* is a stock-simulation game that allows you to trade shares just as you would in a real brokerage account.

Government Agencies

www.irs.gov
www.completetax.com
www.medicare.gov
www.socialsecurity.gov/estimator
www.socialsecurity.gov

Home Based Businesses

U.S. Small Business Administration (800) 827-5722; *sba.gov*

American Home Business Association (866) 396-7773 homebusinessworks.com

Entrepreneur.com is an online small business resource center providing information and advice on products, services and resources.

Familybusinessmagazine.com offers tips, articles and advice about starting and operating a family business.

Home-based-business-opportunities.com features hundreds of home based and small business opportunities listings.

Homebusinessmag.com is an online magazine with information, advice, tools and links for home business owners.

Powerhomebiz.com provides information, advice and tools for home business owners.

Sbomag.com is the Small Business Opportunities Magazine providing readers with the latest small business opportunities news, information and industry resources.

Index Funds

There are literally hundreds of mutual funds that index every segment of the market. Here are two of the better funds to consider: Fidelity Spartan Market Index Fund, which mirrors the Standard & Poor's 500 (S&P 500) index (800-544-8888) T. Rowe Price Equity Index Fund, which mirrors the S&P 500 (800-638-5660).

Industry Trends

ABC News *(www.abcnews.com)* features articles on current industry news and market expert commentary. American Society of Association Executives *(www.asaenet.org)* provides high quality industry overviews including briefings of industry trends. Hoovers Online *(www.stockscreener.com)* offer excellent information on industries at their website. *Research* magazine *(www.researchmag.com)* offers helpful references to industry news, columns, and highlights.

Insurance

If you are paying for your own insurance, go to *www.ehealthinsurance.com*to determine if there is a less expensive plan to switch to. The website at *www.nmfn.com* will help you estimate your life span and need for life insurance based on your age, gender, lifestyle, and medical history.

International Investing

The Internet is rich in sources for information on foreign companies. Three websites in particular with useful information are *www.bankofny.com, wwwjpmorgan.com,* and *www.global-investor.com.* Also, FT Market Watch *(wwwftmarketwatch.com)* provides up-to-the minute news on offshore companies and foreign markets.

Investment Advice

The websites at *www.morningstar.com, www.kiplinger.com,* and *www.investools.com* will help you select stocks and mutual funds that meet your investment parameters. Shop around for the best certificate of deposit rates in your area at *www.bankrate.com.* To learn more about home loans, foreclosure prevention, and predatory lending, go to *www.loansafe.org.* Bankrate.com can find the best rates available in your area for motor vehicles.

Bank of America's website *(www.bankamerica.com)* offers a retirement center under the heading Achieve Your Goals on their main menu. It has several useful references for advice for retirees. Investor Home *(www.investorhome.com)* provides information about the investment process and how to bulletproof your portfolio.

Investment Associations

American Association of Individual Investors *(www.aaii.com)* offers a variety of valuable services to their members, including local chapter meetings in the major metropolitan areas.

The National Association of Investors Corporation (NAIC) is a national association with local chapters throughout the country. Their goal is to help investors develop a disciplined approach to successful investing. For more information, visit their website at *www.better-investing.org*.

Magazines

Business Week (www.businessweek.com) is available online to all of its subscribers.

Forbes (www.forbes. com) is available online and features articles on personal finance and investing.

Fortune (wwwfortune.com) includes special market reports as well as stock and fund quotes.

Kiplinger's (www.kiplinger.com) has a broader scope than many of its competitors. Instead of talking just about investing, *Kiplinger's* moves into other issues of personal business, such as credit card spending, loans, college tuition, and vacation planning. For subscription information, call 800-624-2946.

Newsweek (www.newsweek.com) not only covers the general news but also covers the latest news about the stock market. *SmartMoney* is the" *Wall Street Journal* magazine of personal business" and it's excellent. For subscription information, call 800-444-4204 or visit their website at *www.smartmoney.com*.

Worth columnists, including Peter Lynch, are second to none, and the magazine's regular features are dynamite. For subscription information, call 800-777-1851 or go to *www.worth. com. Money* does an excellent job of keeping its readers informed about what's happening in the mutual fund market. For subscription information, visit their website at *www.money.com.*

Motor Vehicle Acquisition

For comprehensive car-buying information, go to *www.edmunds.com, www.autobytelcom,* and *www.carsmart.com.* To get an estimate of used car values, go to the Kelly Blue Book at *www.kbb.com,* Edmunds at *www.cdmunds.com,* or eAuto at *www.eauto.com.* If you are interested in purchasing a used vehicle, check out:

Trader Online *(www.traderonline.com)*

Kelley Blue Book's Classifieds *(www.kbb.com)*

Online Auto *(www.onlineauto.com)*

Auto Web Interactive *(www.autoweb.com).*

If you are interested in purchasing a new vehicle, check out *www.autosite.com* to find dealer invoice prices or find out about the maintenance records on cars that interest you.

Mutual Fund Companies and Brokers

Charles Schwab *(www.schwab.com)*

Fidelity Investments *(www.jidelity.com)*

T. Rowe Price *(www.troweprice.com)*

Vanguard Group *(www.vanguard.com)*

Mutual Funds

There are almost as many mutual funds to choose from as there are stocks. The following websites will help you find the best ones out there:

CBS Market Watch *(www.marketwatch.com)* provides articles, news, and market data on funds.

MaxFunds *(www.maxfunds.com)* specializes in offering news and statistics on small and little-known funds.

Morningstar *(www.morningstar.com)* is a premier site providing all kinds of information about mutual funds.

Fidelity *(wwwjidelity.com)* offers direct purchase plans for its funds.

Janus *(www.janus. com)* has a family of no-load funds that you can purchase or apply for online.

T. Rowe Price *(www.troweprice.com)* offers direct purchase plans for its funds.

Vanguard *(www.vanguard.com)* has more than eighty funds that you can purchase directly from the company.

News Online

One of the biggest advantages of getting your news online is that you can go to the specific news sector (e.g., Market Watch) without having to thumb through a bunch of paper to get there. Here are several excellent sites to try:

ABC News *(www.abcnews.com)* features business and industry news and market commentary.

Bloomberg Personal Finance *(www.bloomberg.com)* is loaded with timely business news, data, and an analysis of the market.

News Page *(www.newspage.com)* allows you to customize daily news abstracts that it sends to your e-Mail address.

Newspapers

Financial newspapers are still a way of life in the stock market's paper-oriented world, although some of them are beginning to make the migration over to the online sector. Here's a rundown of several excellent papers that are out there:

The *Financial Times (wwwft.com)* provides special reports on the market and the different industry sectors.

Investor's Business Daily is a great financial newspaper that publishes important information to help determine the value of a stock. For subscription information, call 800-831-2525 or visit their website at *www.investors.com.*

The *New York Times (www.nytimes.com)* provides a business section that includes quotes and charts, a portfolio management tool, and breaking business news.

USA Today (www.usatoday.com) features a money section that includes investment articles and news, economic information, and information on industry groups.

The *Wall Street Journal* is the Big Kahuna among investment newspapers, although its authority isn't as unquestioned as it used to be. For subscription information, call 800-778-0840 or visit their website at *www.wsj.com.*

Portfolio Management

There are several portfolio management tools that you can use to manage your portfolio. Check out the following websites:

Morningstar (*www.morningstar.com*) provides a portfolio setup menu that is easy to use.

Quicken *(www.quicken.com)* offers a variety of financial tools including an excellent portfolio-management program.

Microsoft (*www.money.msn.com*) offers a wealth of financial data.

Professional Advice

www.napfa.org
www.fpanet.org
www.aicpa.org

Quotes (Stocks and Mutual Funds)

American Stock Exchange (*www.amex.com)* offers quoting services on their website for stocks that are traded on its exchange.

Microsoft Investor (*www.investor.msn.com)* offers a free stock ticker that you can personalize along with portfolio-tracking tools.

The National Association of Securities Dealers *(www. nasdaq.com)* offers quoting services on their website for stocks that are traded on its exchange.

The New York Stock Exchange *(www.nyse.com)* offers quoting services on their website for stocks that are traded on its exchange.

PC Quote *(www.pcquote.com)* offers current stock prices, portfolio tracker, company profiles, and broker recommendations.

Business Week (www.businessweek.com/investor) features applicable information for researching investment opportunities.

Real Estate

Cost-of-living and moving calculators are available at *http://cgi.money.cnn.com/tools*. To calculate mortgage rates and review *Money* magazine articles on real estate, go to *www.usatoday.comlmoney*. The following websites will provide you with additional information on real estate:

www.bankrate.com
www.realestate.msn.com
www.craigslist.com
www.wheretoretire.com

Reducing Expenses

The following websites will provide you with information about how to reduce expenses:

www.carpoolworld.com
www.erideshares.com
www.campusbookretals.com
www.chegg.com
www.billshrink.com
www.energystar.gov

Retirement Planning

Charles Schwab's website will help you develop a retirement plan with their online calculators, tools, and advice at *www.schwab.com* (click on Advice & Retirement at the top of the menu). Quicken offers a software product called Will Maker that is available at several computer stores and online at *www.nolo.com.*A retirement budget worksheet is available at *wwwjidelity.com* when you select the Retirement & Guidance option in their main menu.

A retirement calculator can be accessed at *www.usnews.com* when you select the Retirement sub-menu that is under their Money & Business main menu. If you are interested in getting an annuity quote, go to *www.immediateannuities.com*. The following websites will provide you with additional information on retirement planning:

www.flexibleretirementPlanner.com
www.immediateannuities.com
www.quicken.com/retirment/planner
www.kinplinger.com
www.smartmoney.com
www.money.com
www.schwab.com
60 Plus Association at *www.60plus.org*
American Association of Retired People at *www.aarp.org*
Fifty Plus at *www.fifty-plus.net*
Grand Times at *www.grandtimes.com*
Hoover's Online *(www.stockscreener.com)* provides a special module for retirement planning.
Information Seniors at *www.infoseniors.com*

Reverse Mortgages

www.aarp.com
www.revmort.com/nrmla

Savings Programs

For steps to take to save money, go to *www.themoneykeys.com*. To determine if you are saving enough, go to *www.kiplinger.com*

Shopping and Selling

If you are shopping for an item or selling a household item that would be difficult to get an appraisal on, see what similar items are selling for in the classified advertisements or on *www.ebay.com, www.netmarket.com,* or *www.craigslist.com.* Yellow Page listings are available at *http://search.bigfoot.com* or *www.switchboard.com.* The following websites will provide you with additional information on shopping and buying on the internet:

www.bluefly.com
www.yoox.com

Stock and Mutual Fund Market Timing

The following websites will provide you with additional information on timing the stock and mutual fund markets:

www.schwab.com
www.trowprice.com
vanguard.com
www.fidelity.com
www.fundalarm.com
www.timingthemarket.net
www.stockcharts.com
www.vectorvest.com

Stock Evaluation Programs

Finding out what stock analysts are saying about a stock that you're considering can help you determine if it's the right time to buy. Here are several sites that will get you the information you need:

VectorVest *(www.vectorvest.com)* offers free reports showing what your stocks are really worth, how safe they are, and when to buy, sell, or hold. It's one of the best analyst's sites on the Internet.

S&P Advisor Insight *(www.advisorinsight.com)* allows you to review Standard & Poor's reports for major stocks.

Zacks Investment Research *(www.zacks.com)* reports on what analysts are saying about most of the stocks on the U.S. exchanges.

Stock Exchanges

The American, NASDAQ and New York Stock Exchanges offer a wide variety of investment features that may appeal to you.

American Stock Exchange *(www.amex.com)*.

The National Association of Securities Dealers *(www. nasdaq.com)*.

The New York Stock Exchange *(www.nyse.com)*.

Taxes

For tax deductions, go to *www.bottomlinesecrets.comlextra*. For tax preparation ideas, go to *http://tax.yahoo.comlchecklist.html*.

Travel Websites

www.expedia.com

www.travelocity.com

www.besifares.com

www.budgettravel.com

Web Search Engines

Alta Vista: *www.altavista.com*

Google: *www.google.com*

HotBot: *www.hotbot.com*

Lycos: *uruno.lycos.com*

Yahoo!: *www.yahoo.com*

About The Author and Testimonials

David Rye was the founder of Computech Corporation and later, a director at IBM where he earned an MBA with honors from Seattle University. He is currently president of Western Publications and writes personal finance books from his Goodyear, Arizona office. His award-winning books include *It's Not Too Late To Rescue Your 401(k)*, *Stop Managing and Lead*, *Starting Up*, and *1001 Way to Inspire Yourself*. He also consultants baby boomers to show them how to get the most out of their retirement plans.

"Perfect for boomers who are about to retire and are thinking about retiring ... in a standard of living they can be comfortable with."

Dr. T.K. Nelsen, Stanford University

"A great book in a writing style that is highly interactive where each chapter challenges to reader to expand their role in retirement ... you'll learn how you can retire in $tyle."

Dale Moser, President and CEO, Niwot Technology, Inc.

"A hands-on book that dramatically illustrates how anyone can enjoy life after they retire."

Mark Kruger, Ph.D., Creative Thinking Seminars

"... adds an element of real world reality to the retirement process that is truly unique and refreshing."

A.J. Osorio, President, Llanos Publishing